Politics, Policy and Practice in Physical Education

Politics, Policy and Practice in Physical Education

Dawn Penney and John Evans

Taylor & Francis
Taylor & Francis Group

LONDON AND NEW YORK

First published 1999 by Taylor & Francis
Reprinted 2003
By Taylor & Francis
2 Park Square, Milton Park, Abingdon, Oxon, OX14 4RN
Transferred to Digital Printing 2006

Typeset in Ssabon by The Florence Group, Stoodleigh, Devon

British Library Cataloguing in Publication Data
A catalogue record for this book is available from the British Library

Library of Congress Cataloging in Publication Data
Penney, Dawn, 1966–
   Politics, policy, and practice in physical education / Dawn Penney
and John Evans.
      p. cm.
   Includes bibliographical references and index.
   1. Physical education and training–England–Curriculum.
2. Physical education and training–Wales–Curriculum.   3. Physical
education and training–Political aspects–England.   4. Physical
education and training–Political aspects–Wales.   5. Curriculum
planning–England.   6. Curriculum planning–Wales   I. Evans, John,
1952 Oct. 16–   .   II. Title.
GV363.P45   1999
613.7'071'042–dc21   98–38800
                                                          CIP

ISBN 0–419–21950–1

Publisher's Note

Contents

Acknowledgements

The research on which this book draws has been the subject of three major research grants, from the Sports Council (1990–1993), the Economic and Social Research Council (ESRC) (1992–1994; project reference No. ROO 23 3629), and the Leverhulme Trust (1994–1996; project reference No. F1800). We are grateful to these organisations for their support and to the universities in which we have been employed while conducting and writing about this research; the University of Southampton, Loughborough University, the University of Queensland and De Montfort University.

The book draws upon material presented in Penney's (1994) unpublished doctoral thesis:

Penney, D. (1994) '"NO CHANGE IN A NEW ERA?" The Impact of the Education Reform Act (1988) on the Provision of PE and Sport in State Schools', PhD thesis, University of Southampton.

and material published in a number of academic journals during the course of our research. We are therefore grateful to the journals and publishers concerned for supporting our bringing together of this work in what we hope is an informative and thought provoking text.

Material from the following publications is reproduced with the kind permission of the journals and publishers concerned:

Penney, D. and Evans, J. (1991) 'The Impact of the Education Reform Act (ERA) on the Provision of Physical Education and Sport in the 5–16 Curriculum of State Schools', *British Journal of Physical Education* 22(1): 38–42.

Evans, J. and Penney, D. with Bryant, A. (1993) 'Physical Education after ERA', *British Journal of Physical Education Research Supplement* no. 13 (Autumn): 2–5.

Evans, J., Penney, D. and Bryant, A. (1993) 'Theorising Implementation: A Preliminary Comment on Power and Process in Policy Research', *Physical Education Review* 16(1): 5–22.

Evans, J., Penney, D. and Bryant, A. (1993) 'Playing by Market Rules: Physical Education in England and Wales after ERA', in G. McFee and A. Tomlinson (eds) *Education, Sport, Leisure: Connections and Controversies*. Eastbourne: Chelsea School Research Centre, University of Brighton.

Evans, J., Davies, B. and Penney, D. (1994) 'Whatever Happened to the Subject and the State in Policy Research in Education', *Discourse: Studies in the Cultural Politics of Education*, 14(2): 57–64.

Evans, J. and Penney, D. (1995) 'Physical Education, Restoration and the Politics of Sport', *Curriculum Studies* 3(2): 183–196.

Evans, J. and Penney, D. (1995) 'The Politics of Pedagogy: making a National Curriculum Physical Education', *Journal of Education Policy* 10(1): 27–44. (Published by the Taylor & Francis Group Ltd.)

Penney, D. and Evans, J. (1995) 'Changing Structures: Changing Rules: The Development of the "Internal Market"', *School Organisation* 15(1): 13–21. (*School Organisation* is now entitled *School Leadership & Management* and is published by Carfax Publishing Limited, PO Box 25, Abingdon, Oxfordshire OX14 3UE, UK.)

Penney, D. and Evans, J. (1996) 'When Breadth and Balance means Balancing the Books: Curriculum Planning in Schools post-ERA', in C. Pole and R. Chawla (eds) *Educational Change in the 1990s: Perspectives on Secondary Schooling*. London: Falmer Press.

Penney, D. and Evans, J. (1997) 'Naming the Game. Discourse and Domination in Physical Education and Sport in England and Wales', *European Physical Education Review*, 3(1): 21–32.

Material is also reprinted by permission from Evans, J., Penney, D. and Bryant, A. (1993) 'Improving the Quality of Physical Education? The Education Reform Act 1988 and Physical Education in England and Wales', *Quest*, 45(3): 321–338.

Material reproduced from Penney, D. and Evans, J. (1994) 'From "Policy" to "Practice": the Development and Implementation of the National Curriculum for Physical Education', in D. Scott (ed.) *Accountability and Control in Educational Settings* is by permission of Cassell plc, Wellington House, 125 Strand, London, England.

Abbreviations

ACAC	Awdurod Cwricwlwm Asesu Cymru (Curriculum and Assessment Authority for Wales)
BAALPE	British Association of Advisers and Lecturers in Physical Education
BCPE	British Council of Physical Education
BISC	British Institute of Sports Coaches
CCPR	Central Council of Physical Recreation
CCW	Cyngor Cwricwlwm Cymru (Curriculum Council for Wales)
DES	Department of Education and Science
DFE	Department for Education
DNH	Department of National Heritage
ERA	Education Reform Act
ESC	English Sports Council
GCSE	General Certificate of Secondary Education
GMS	Grant-Maintained status
HEA	Health Education Authority
HRE	Health related exercise
HRF	Health related fitness
INSET	In-service educational training
LEA	Local Education Authority
LMS	Local management of schools
NCC	National Curriculum Council
NCF	National Coaching Foundation
NCPE	National Curriculum for Physical Education
OFSTED	Office for Standards in Education
OHMCI	Office of Her Majesty's Chief Inspector of Schools in Wales
PE	Physical education
PEA	Physical Education Association
SCOPE	Standing Conference on Physical Education in Teacher Education
SEAC	Schools Examinations and Assessment Council
SCAA	School Curriculum and Assessment Authority
WO	Welsh Office
YST	Youth Sport Trust

Preface: about this book

Between 1988 and 1997 a plethora of policy initiatives emanating from Conservative central governments in the United Kingdom (UK) served to highlight, perhaps as never before, the contested nature of education and physical education (PE) in schools. During these years it became apparent that there was profound disagreement about what education and physical education should look like in content and form, and what and whose purposes they should serve. Rhetorically, the explicit intent of government policies was to 'raise standards' in education by injecting free market principles (essentially 'competition and greater accountability') into all arenas of the education systems of England and Wales. The Education Reform Act 1988 (ERA), which included among its measures the development of a National Curriculum for state (i.e. government-funded) schools in England and Wales, was to be the main means of achieving this ideal. However, the development of the National Curriculum showed that inherent in the ERA's requirements were interests and values that were neither arbitrary, accidental nor insignificant, culturally or politically. Embedded in the National Curriculum were views and directives relating to what it meant to be physically educated and what forms of behaviour, attitude, identity and citizenship the curriculum should promote. The view, perhaps widespread in the public mind, that physical education and sport are politically neutral activities, was patently laid bare as it became clear that political interests were as much at stake in the worlds of physical education and sport as they are in all other areas of the curriculum in schools.

In addition to highlighting this lack of neutrality in education and physical education, contemporary policies demonstrated the significance of the distinction between **physical education** and **sport**. As we show in subsequent chapters, in the UK the relationship between physical education and sport has been a recurring issue in debates and disputes within the physical education profession and between it, the media and politicians. In these debates the distinctive purposes and the practices of physical education have been obfuscated and marginalised, often intentionally, in the light of other political interests and desires, and particularly the interests of competitive, elite sport (see Kay 1998).

While events in the UK have illustrated the contested identity and purpose of physical education particularly vividly, neither these matters nor the structural and ideological changes in education as a whole, are concerns that are unique to the UK. They are, at least in part, reflections of socio-economic and cultural changes and developments occurring on a global terrain. The issues of who and what are defining physical education and controlling the purposes that it serves, and of how particular definitions and elements of 'control' of teaching and learning are being established and reinforced, are matters for those involved in physical education world-wide to address. They are issues that have been central to the research upon which this book is based.

We acknowledge that no understanding of physical education is complete without a historical view of the relationships between past and present practices (see Kirk 1992) or of the relationships between education, the economy and the state. Nevertheless, in this text we centre our attention upon the contemporary struggles between central government and educationalists in England and Wales to define physical education in schools, and upon how and why particular definitions emerged as dominant in a National Curriculum for physical education. It is the characteristics of this process of struggle that are our ongoing focus and particular concern. The book is, therefore, a study in the sociology and politics of knowledge in physical education. It explores the complex relationship between policy and practice in education and the influence of political agendas and interests in determining what is defined as worthwhile knowledge in physical education and how it is to be evaluated and taught. At times our discussion and analysis may well seem dense, but we urge readers to persevere with what in our view, are important concepts for those concerned with critical thinking and progressive developments in physical education to embrace. As little has been written about the contemporary politics of knowledge in physical education in schools either in the UK or elsewhere, we also hope that the text will go some way towards filling a gap in the literature in physical education. We share Graham's view that:

> It is high time to take the lid off, to lift the veil gently and confirm your worst fears, albeit with a chuckle and a wry smile. Perhaps you will then be better able to understand the game and possibly better equipped to deal with it.
>
> (1996: xii)

In pursuing the matters of the contested nature of knowledge and curricula we also draw attention to issues of **equity and justice** that are at the heart of our own concern for progress in physical education. These are issues that are of relevance not only to physical educationalists, but to all interested in advancing the cause of social progress in schools and the societies that they serve. Our hope is that wherever they are based, physical educationalists and others reading this text may find it a useful resource for critical reflection upon contemporary developments in education, a source of ideas for innovation in the field, and a means of assessing whether or not a newly marketised education system helps to promote or eradicate an agenda for equity in education policy and practice in schools.

In Chapter 1 we explain the empirical context of our research and in so doing set the scene for subsequent discussion and analysis. We outline the changes to both the content and context of education in England and Wales that were the catalyst for our own work and for the development of a body of research and literature concerned with education policy. We identify our particular interests relating to the development of a National Curriculum for physical education, discuss the implications of these research interests for the nature and focus of our subsequent inquiries and address a number of methodological issues central to policy research. We emphasise the contested nature of physical education and our anticipation that attempts to define it in the development of a National Curriculum would be far from simple.

From this point on readers may well choose different paths through the text and/or be selective in their reading. In particular, not all may wish to pursue the theorising of policy and curriculum development that is our focus in Chapters 2 and 7. Instead they may choose to go straight to the detail of the contestation in the development of policy and practice in physical education in England and Wales in the 1990s, presented in Chapters 3, 4, 5 and 6.

Chapter 2, then, is concerned with the theoretical issues that have occupied our attention in recent years and that are likely to confront all who venture on to the field of policy research. Specifically we explore the nature of the relationship between 'policy' and 'practice'; policy 'making' and 'implementation', and highlight some of the shortcomings in the ways in which these concepts have traditionally been defined and understood. We develop a view of policy as a socio-cultural and political **process**, and in so doing deconstruct what in our view are unhelpful conceptual dichotomies that do little to clarify the challenging complexity of policy and curriculum development in schools. We emphasise the importance of both texts and contexts, and the relationships between them, in shaping what (physical) education looks like in policy and practice. We also stress the active role that *many* sites in education systems play in both the making and implementation of policy. This chapter therefore provides an important foundation for our subsequent illustration of the policy process and its complexities in our description and critique of the development and implementation of the National Curriculum for Physical Education (NCPE) in England and Wales.

Chapters 3, 4, 5 and 6 provide this empirical illustration and analysis of the policy process. These chapters explore the complexity of relationships between various sites of policy action and educational practice and the different roles, authority and influence of individuals involved in the making and implementation of the NCPE in state schools in England and Wales between 1990 and 1995. Individually and together the chapters highlight how important it is to understand physical education 'relationally'; that is to say as socially constructed, not only by the interactions of teachers and students inside physical education 'classrooms', but also by the range of influences and actions of many others operating outside classrooms, in other arenas of education, the state and civil society. In documenting this process, we highlight the *particular* values and interests at play in the development of the policy and practice of physical education in England and Wales and draw attention to key people and factors influencing the form and content of teaching and learning in this subject. We show how narrow definitions of physical education 'as sport' have been privileged in the development of the NCPE and how difficult it has been for alternative, perhaps more progressive definitions of physical education to be voiced or expressed in either policy or practice.

In Chapters 3 and 4 our descriptions and inquiries centre upon the **national** dimension of the policy process. We analyse the production of the 'official texts' of the NCPE for England and Wales issued by consecutive Conservative central governments and their aides, that set out the requirements for physical education that all state schools have been legally required to implement. Our analysis examines 'who had what say' in the making of the texts, what definitions of physical education were provided by them, the values and interests expressed in these definitions and how particular ('restorationist' 'back to basic') values and interests came to be privileged over and above others. We highlight the political influences at play in this development and the significance of the relative power and authority of central government in determining the form and content of the texts produced. We describe the way in which these influences became increasingly explicit in the development of the NCPE and how, in turn, the agenda for the further development of the subject became progressively narrowed. Chapter 4 in particular stands out as being long, but we felt that it was important to follow through key themes in our analysis without undue breaks in our own text.

In Chapter 5 we examine the role of **local government** in the making and implementation of the texts formulated at a national level. We identify Local Education Authorities (LEAs) in England and Wales as key sites 'between' central government and schools and examine their ability to mediate, adopt and/or resist directives and interests from both 'above' and 'below'. Our data suggest that LEAs achieved notable but by no means absolute power in relation to policy. They held an influential position that the central government openly sought to undermine. Once again we highlight the dynamic between policies and the contexts in which they are developed and in parallel take a critical look at the views of physical education being reinforced in the policy process. We explore the complex range of factors underlying the privileging of particular interests and subordination of others.

In Chapter 6 we turn our attention to **schools and physical education teachers**. We identify significant constraints to teachers' involvement in the development of the NCPE in England and Wales and the limited potential and support for curriculum development in the context of market-driven education systems. At the same time, however, we highlight the way in which schools and teachers remain key arenas and figures in the policy process and show that micro political conditions and organisational arrangements within schools are critical in shaping the expression of policy 'in practice'. We therefore emphasise that despite the drift towards centralisation in education policy, schools and teachers continue to play a critical role in determining what constitutes physical education, whose needs and interests it serves and who it ignores or excludes, albeit within increasingly restrictive frames of legislation and resource.

In Chapter 7 we return to the matter of how we might make sense of and theorise policy as we reflect upon the complexities of policy making and implementation, and the inequalities inherent and so visible in the policy process. How different sites and the individuals located within them are positioned socially and politically in the policy process are matters that are at the heart of our discussion of 'autonomy', 'control' and 'power' in relation to policy and practice in education. We point to the difficulties in developing a conceptual framework that embraces the subtleties of the macro and micro processes addressed in this text, and pursue our understandings of 'power' and 'reform' in relation to education policy. We debate the extent of the space and potential that remains in the ongoing development of the NCPE for 'resistance' in the policy process; for the privileging of 'alternative' discourses that to date have been marginalised and subordinated in both the texts and contexts of schooling and in wider society. This provides the basis for us to return in Chapter 8 to our concern with the nature of physical education in schools and the values that it expresses and promotes.

In Chapter 8 we therefore turn attention to **future directions in physical education**, particularly in England and Wales, but also elsewhere. We discuss the position and representation of various discourses 'within' and 'of' physical education and the National Curriculum for Physical Education and discuss potential 'alternative' readings of official policies. We assess the ways in which we may explore 'gaps' in policies of physical education and thus redefine and/or redirect their thrust and intent. In conclusion we explain that the practices that constitute a National Curriculum for Physical Education in England and Wales are still emerging and evolving. Indeed, further changes are being made to statutory requirements. We point to the need for teaching and curriculum development in physical education to be grounded in ongoing research and emphasise the potential for research to actively inform both policy and practice in physical education. We hope that this text will promote interest in such research and further critique of policies and practices of physical education. In particular we hope that it will presage greater awareness and understanding of the complexities of the policy process in education and provide important insights into the restrictions on, but also potential for, the progressive development of physical education and sport in schools. This text comes at a time when teachers in England and Wales are once again faced with pending changes to the National Curriculum, now under a Labour rather than Conservative central government. It may therefore also help provide some means of assessing whether New Labour's education policies are any more likely than their Conservative predecessors to help teachers develop an agenda for equity and deliver forms of physical education that leave children and young people better able to meet the changing sociocultural conditions, relations and requirements of a post modern age.

Chapter 1

Introduction: background to the policy game

The 1980s and 1990s were turbulent years for teachers and all others concerned with the provision of education in state schools in England and Wales. Repeatedly, schools and teachers were subjected to vitriolic critique from Conservative politicians and their supporting tabloid popular press. By all accounts there was something badly wrong with state education and an urgent need for central government to act to correct this state of affairs. These claims bore little resemblance to what was going on in schools or what research evidence had revealed were the challenges for and successes of comprehensive schools (Hammersley 1994; Simon 1988). The Education Reform Act (ERA), passed by the British parliament in 1988 was not the first piece of legislation to emerge from Conservative central government at the time, but rather it represented a high point of the government's project to deal with the 'crisis' in state education in England and Wales, and to transform both its content and form. The ERA also served as an announcement that from this time on there would be increasingly more direct central government intervention in the provision of education in state schools in England and Wales. No longer would teachers and other educationalists enjoy privileged control over the curriculum in schools. In the government's view the 'crisis' and 'decline in standards' in education prevailed across all aspects of the state education system. Furthermore, it was seen as being brought on by ideologically driven 'progressive' (which was usually meant to imply 'politically left wing') teaching, putatively endemic in the system, and by virtue of teacher (producer) control of the curriculum taking precedence over parents' (consumers) interests. With a general election pending, the government needed to be seen to be addressing 'the nation's problems'. Responding to this 'crisis in education' had clear potential to be a vote winner (Davies, Holland and Minhas 1990), with education promoted as the key to ameliorating all Britain's social and economic ills.

The ERA

It was always evident that the scale and scope of the ERA's reform of education would be great. It was an Act that on the one hand made fundamental changes to the arrangements for the funding and operation of state schools in England and Wales, and on the other, via the development and introduction of a National Curriculum, established the foundations for a redefinition of the education that they would provide. The Act thus comprised two distinct but critically interrelated parts; one addressing the **context** of the provision of education in state schools in England and Wales; the other the **content** of that education. It also brought to the fore critical questions in education; in particular of what education is about, whose interests it serves and what the curriculum in schools should therefore look like. In some respects the Act, and in particular the introduction of a National Curriculum, could be seen as presenting important opportunities for reflection on and development of school curricula, and a move towards greater standardisation in relation to the experiences that pupils in different schools would enjoy. Indeed, the idea of a National Curriculum was warmly, if cautiously, welcomed by individuals from across the political spectrum and within and outside of the teaching profession. The contentious issue that remained was who should decide what the content of a National Curriculum should be? At a time when trends were towards centralisation, the fear was that teachers and other educationalists (for example from Local Education Authorities, further and higher education) would have little say as to the direction that developments should take. As we will see, these fears were fully justified.

At the same time as confronting questions about what the curriculum should and would look like, schools faced the prospect of delivering new curricula under notably different conditions and rules. The ERA set out the timetable for the introduction of measures directed towards greater efficiency and accountability in a new competitive education system. Pupil intake numbers were to have direct financial implications for schools, and school performance was destined to be judged by pupils' results in standardised programmes of testing. Long-standing restrictions on enrolments were dissolved by the ERA (see p. 8), and thus, it was predicted that the successful schools would survive and prosper in the education market, while those failing to attract adequate pupils would face closure (see for example Ball 1990a).

It was in this context that our interest in the future of physical education in England and Wales was set. Like many others in education at this time, our research interests were stimulated by the ERA. What would the prospects and opportunities be for physical education after the ERA? What would a National Curriculum for Physical Education (NCPE) look like – as a 'policy' but also as 'practice' in schools operating under these market rules? Consecutive Conservative governments had identified physical education as a central concern in relation to both the nation's international standing and its social well being. It was claimed that physical education typified everything that was wrong with state education in the UK and that physical education was riddled with progressive elements that needed to be removed if Britain was to regain its rightful place on the international sporting stage (see Evans 1990; Evans and Penney 1995a). There was clear recognition of the potential for physical education to play a role in putting the 'Great' back into Britain, and in socialisation and social control.

Our interests certainly went further than merely documenting what children ultimately received as a National Curriculum for Physical Education. The complexity and the openly political nature of the act (see Kay 1998; Simon 1988) and the conditions that it looked set to create in the education system begged investigation of how and why these outcomes ultimately took the particular form that they did. The ERA privileged the Conservative party's New Right ideologies of cultural restorationism, competitive individualism and free market principles (see Evans and Penney 1995a), and as we explain further below (see pp. 5–6), established particular arrangements for the development and implementation of its policies. These latter characteristics ensured that the Conservative government's agendas would remain dominant throughout. Our ambitions therefore lay in documenting and analysing the processes of the development and implementation of the NCPE and, specifically, unpacking the particular form that it took, both as a policy document and as practice in schools. Inherent in this interest was a desire to see progress and, particularly, moves towards greater equality and equity in education and physical education (see Evans 1993). With others in the physical education profession we felt that the introduction of a National Curriculum was an important opportunity to both consolidate some of the more innovative ideas that had found their way into physical education in the 1970s and 1980s, such as the introduction of health related exercise, new forms of games teaching and co-educational PE (see for example Armstrong and Sparkes 1991; Evans 1986) and also to assess the need for further shifts in thinking and practice in the subject. We also realised, however, that there was certainly no guarantee of such progress. The making of the curriculum would be a matter of contestation within and beyond the profession and it was always questionable whether the conditions of schools and schooling created by the ERA would support fulfilment of the stated aims of the National Curriculum 'to take forward more quickly, and more comprehensively across the country, the achievement of consistently high standards' and to ensure that 'good curriculum practice is much more widely employed' (Department of Education and Science (DES) 1989a, 3.1).

Below we outline the ERA's key policies that were central to our research. In so doing we explore both the opportunities for and potential threats to the future development of physical education in England and Wales. The descriptions of the ERA's policies of local management of schools (LMS), open enrolment, grant-maintained status (GMS) and the planned development of a National Curriculum provide essential background to our subsequent focus on the National Curriculum for Physical Education. As we will see, these policies incorporated in the ERA were critical in creating particular conditions in which the NCPE was made and implemented in schools, and an appreciation of them is therefore a necessary prerequisite to understanding the events that followed in the development and implementation of the NCPE. We also provide a brief commentary on our research, pointing in particular to the nature of the data that we have drawn upon in our writing, the limitations of our research and methodological issues that have arisen in the course of our work. Again our hope is that these are issues which will be of interest not only in the context of physical education studies, but also in other areas of education and policy studies.

The National Curriculum

The ERA legislated for the development of a National Curriculum that all state schools in England and Wales would be legally required to introduce. Specifically it outlined the form and structure of the curriculum 'as a whole', and the framework to be adopted in the development of each of the identified National Curriculum subjects. Subjects, each treated as a discrete area of knowledge, were the primary focus in defining the National Curriculum. While it is easy to regard this as 'obvious' and 'only natural', we draw attention to it because it is not the only focus that could have been adopted. Cross-curricular issues, such as personal and social education, gender and multi-cultural issues, were identified as a component of the whole curriculum but not part of the statutory National Curriculum (see DES 1989a). These *could* have provided the basis for a curriculum that emphasised different educational concerns and values to those inherent in and promoted by subject-focused studies (see Chapter 3).

The model presented by the ERA was thus a curriculum comprising **core and foundation subjects**. English, mathematics and science, and in Welsh-speaking schools in Wales, Welsh, were identified as the core subjects. Technology, history, geography, art, music, physical education and a modern foreign language, and in non-Welsh speaking schools in Wales, Welsh, were the foundation subjects. Development of each of these subjects centred on the identification of (i) **Attainment Targets** covering 'the range of knowledge, skills and understanding that pupils should be expected and helped to master as they progress through school' and offering 'general objectives, setting out areas within which pupils will need to develop their attainments' (DES 1989a, 3.11–3.12); and (ii) **Programmes** of Study setting out 'the essential matters, skills and processes which need to be covered by pupils at each stage of their education' (ibid., 3.12). In addition it was planned that orders would contain 'statements of attainment', describing up to ten levels of attainment and providing the basis for the assessment arrangements for the National Curriculum. Assessment was identified as 'an integral part of the National Curriculum' (ibid., 6.1) and establishing requirements for the formal assessment of student learning was a move clearly designed to provide the government and parents alike with 'an obvious' measure of school performance.

The programmes of study and the formal assessment were structured around four key stages of education established for the National Curriculum. Key stages 1 and 2 embraced the primary years of education. Key stage 1 comprised a reception year and years 1 and year 2 (ages 5–7), and key stage 2 comprised years 3 to 6 (ages 7–11). Secondary education was similarly divided, with key stage 3 including years 3 to 6 (ages 7–11) and key stage 4, years 10 and 11 (ages 14–16). It was planned that pupils' performance in relation to attainment targets would be assessed and reported upon at the ages of 7, 11, 14 and 16, that different levels of attainment would be registered according to a ten point scale, and that 'standard assessment tasks' (SATs) would be drawn up for teachers to utilise in their formal assessment (DES 1989a). However, as we discuss further in later chapters, these proposals became unmanageable in implementation and were the subject of contestation and modification (see Dearing 1993). It was also notable that different assessment requirements were established for different National Curriculum subjects, seemingly reflecting perceptions about the respective status of different subjects (see Chapter 3).

The ERA therefore established a highly technical and technicist language for the curriculum. This formed a 'discursive frame', effectively defining how teachers and all others concerned with education were now to think, talk and describe practice and performance in schools. However, as we discuss in subsequent chapters, it became increasingly difficult to see what else was new or innovatory in the proposed curriculum. Beneath the surface rhetoric of radical educational change and the new language of and for the curriculum, the National Curriculum quite clearly sought to (re-)establish a traditional curriculum centring on the directed learning of specified knowledge. It became very evident that the definition of the curriculum would not be left to chance, nor would there be much that was new (see also Graham with Tytler 1993). Here we touch upon another critical feature of the ERA; the way in which it detailed the specific arrangements for the development and implementation of the policies that it encompassed. The ERA established two new quangos (quasi autonomous non-governmental organisations) to oversee first, the development and implementation of the National Curriculum, and second, its assessment

arrangements. The National Curriculum Council (NCC) was responsible for the former; the Schools Examinations and Assessment Council
(SEAC) for the latter. Our concerns centre primarily upon the actions of
the NCC. In conjunction with subject working groups, the NCC was
to advise the Secretary of State for Education[1] on the attainment targets
and programmes of study for the National Curriculum subjects (DES
1989a). Notably, the NCC, SEAC and the working groups were comprised
of individuals appointed by the Secretary of State, and were bound by
terms of reference drawn up by the government. In the chapters that
follow we see that these arrangements were far from politically neutral
or value free. Rather, they were critical in ensuring that particular ideological interests were included and privileged in the development, while
others were excluded and/or subordinated. The writings of the ex-chair
of the NCC, Duncan Graham, have clearly indicated that the contestation, processes and inequities that we address in the making of the National
Curriculum for Physical Education were far from unique to this subject.
Rather, political interests and agendas quite openly came into play in the
formulation of many parts of the National Curriculum (see Graham with
Tytler 1993; Graham 1996).

Assigning status to subjects

One of the important features of the arrangements detailed in the ERA
was the specification of a timetable for the development of the National
Curriculum subjects. Significantly this reinforced the distinction between
core and foundation subjects, but also announced a hierarchy among the
various foundation subjects. Implementation of the core subjects was to
commence in September 1989, followed by the introduction of design and
technology in 1990, geography and history in 1991, modern languages,
music, art and physical education in 1992 (DES 1989a). The National
Curriculum thus effectively legitimated and reinforced the low status
historically accorded to the latter subjects. However, this timetable also
had other more practical implications and shortcomings. To a great extent
these stemmed from the fact that while prescribing the subjects to be
incorporated in the National Curriculum and addressing the content to
be pursued in each at each key stage, the time that schools should devote
to the various subjects could not be stipulated. With requirements then
developed on a subject-by-subject basis with very limited communication
and collaboration between groups, it quickly became apparent that too
many claims would be made for the limited time available within schools

---

1 Subsequently in the text we refer to the Secretary of State for Education as the Secretary
  of State.

(Graham with Tytler 1993). As each subject working group outlined what, in their view, was the critical subject matter to be addressed in their subject, those subjects arriving at the end of the development process moved from a position of apparent strength and security as foundation subjects, with a clear contribution to make to the curriculum, to one in which their development seemed threatened by the recognition that the growing demands of the National Curriculum were over-stretching school timetables and resources. In subsequent chapters we see the effects of these conditions on the development of the NCPE, that serve to illustrate the important interaction between policies in the development process, and between texts and the contexts of their production and implementation.

'Playing by market rules': local management of schools, open enrolment and grant-maintained status

The 'other side' of the ERA was concerned with applying market principles to the organisation and operation of educational institutions. Below we outline the three policies that together moved schools to a position of competing with one another for an intake of pupils that would ensure their survival in this education market, and that encouraged further moves towards business orientated approaches in schools' operations. These policies very clearly expressed the Conservative government's ideological belief that 'competition' could and should feature as prominently in education as it did in industry. The policies have been the focus of attention of many researchers and commentators on the ERA and are therefore the subject of a significant body of literature (see for example Ball 1990b; Simon 1988; Maclure 1989). Many writers have directed attention to the political, ideological and economic matters underpinning these policies, some highlighting in particular the 'rationalist' economic agenda of the New Right, and others pointing to similarities between developments in the United Kingdom and those occurring in education in other countries and in particular, the USA (see for example, Apple 1993; Kennedy 1995). Although there have been some important differences in the developments in other countries, many features of the initiatives and conditions that we describe will, it seems, be familiar to teachers world-wide (see for example Sullivan 1997).

Local management of schools (LMS)

LMS addressed the financial and management structure of education in England and Wales. The policy was portrayed as representing an important shift in control of the resourcing of education, with individual schools taking charge of funding previously retained within Local Education

Authorities (LEAs). Specifically, school governing bodies (including parents, teachers and representatives of schools' senior management) were given responsibility for the allocation of funds within their school, including moneys for staff appointments and salaries. This move, termed 'delegated management', was portrayed by central government as presenting schools with new freedom and control over their own operations, and as establishing arrangements whereby responsibility and accountability for 'success' or 'failure' lay openly with individual schools. The intentions of LMS were, quite clearly, to see schools 'run and managed like businesses with a primary focus on the profit and loss account', with 'governors as Board of Directors and headteacher as Chief Executive' (Ball 1990a: 11).

In parallel, LMS incorporated measures that would mean that the number of pupils enrolled at a school would be a key determinant of the school's financial resources. The logic was simple; to survive and prosper in the education market schools would have to attract a sufficient intake of pupils. The ERA thus outlined requirements for 'formula funding'; the allocation of funds to schools primarily on the basis of a formula in which the key criteria were the age and number of pupils at the school (see DES 1988). To create 'open competition' between schools, the ERA also removed the LEAs' long-standing ability to determine the annual maximum intake of schools and thereby to manage the distribution of pupils between schools. Under 'open enrolment' parental choice would act as the new market mechanism by which the distribution of pupils would be determined (see Maclure 1989). The accompanying development of national tests for the National Curriculum would provide parents with 'a simple and crude but direct point of comparison between schools' (Ball 1990a: 11). Published league tables of examination results would provide measures of a school's relative failure or success. There was no recognition of the different potential particular schools have to succeed by these criteria, to 'play well' under market rules. Neither history nor social and geographical context, factors that inevitably have an important bearing upon a school's capacity to achieve high ratings in examination league tables and in turn be 'credible' and 'desirable' in parents' and pupils' eyes, were to be acknowledged or incorporated in the equation for determining 'failure' and 'success'. The playing field was assumed, in the ERA, to be level and fair.

Grant-Maintained schools: the 'independent business'

For some schools, headteachers and school governing bodies, the rhetoric of LMS and open enrolment was attractive. The ERA incorporated further measures to appeal to these people and to encourage the adoption of a business orientation in education. Schools were to be able to keep income generated from the use of their facilities outside school hours (see Chapter 5), and they were also presented with the opportunity of 'opting out' of LEA 'control' and instead attaining grant-maintained status (GMS), then receiving their funding directly from central government rather than via the LEA (Maclure 1989). To go down this entrepreneurial path, school governing bodies were required to ballot parents. Again the emphasis was on the greater freedom and autonomy that the ERA's policies offered schools in relation to their finances and internal organisation. However, we should also note that by bypassing LEAs, these arrangements placed central government in a position from which it could far more easily influence and/or direct the affairs of individual schools. Thus, within a rhetoric of decentralisation lay the new structural opportunity for greater centralisation.

Local Education Authorities

Much to the frustration of the Conservative government few schools took up this opportunity to opt out of LEA 'control'. Certainly (and as we discuss in more detail in Chapter 5), the influence of LEAs was by no means totally diminished or dissolved after the ERA (see also Gerwitz, Ball and Bowe 1995). The ERA required all LEAs to submit 'LMS schemes' which had to incorporate the allocation of the majority of funds on the basis of a pupil driven formula. However, LEAs retained some scope to direct resourcing towards specific aspects of education. They could identify 'discretionary exceptions' that would be funded separately. In addition, in designing their formula they could ensure that funding would take *some* account of the different circumstances and needs of individual schools. Not all funding had to be driven by the criterion of pupil numbers (see DES 1988). In Chapter 5 we illustrate the significance of this flexibility in relation to the resourcing of physical education and, specifically, schools' implementation of the NCPE.

Perhaps more significantly, LEAs also remained the primary source of advice and support for schools faced with the task of delivering the National Curriculum. To opt out of the financial association with an LEA was also to jeopardise the ability to draw on and benefit from the support that it could offer. Breaking this association could also put at risk valuable links with schools and teachers that remained within the LEA structure and control. Schools' rejection of GMS therefore signalled the value of local collaboration between schools, teachers and Local Education Authority staff, and a desire to retain communication and the sharing of expertise within the imposed context of market competition.

The rhetoric of the ERA and LMS in particular was thus of increased freedom and autonomy for schools in this education market. Omitted from this rhetoric was acknowledgement that schools were given responsibility for and control of *limited* and in many cases inadequate resources (see also Bowe and Ball with Gold 1992). This clearly had an important bearing upon their opportunities to enjoy the new freedoms accorded to them. In addition, there was an inherent tension between the two 'sides' of the ERA. While LMS and open enrolment emphasised autonomy and independence in state education (reflecting the discourse of *laissez faire* idealism espoused by neo-liberals within the Conservative party), the National Curriculum presaged standardisation and centralisation (reflecting the more collective, neo-conservative ideals, see also Apple 1993). The balance between the freedom of schools to shape the curricula, and central government control of provision, is an issue that is central to our discussions in subsequent chapters.

Researchers in the policy game

Research attempting to encompass the package of policies that comprised the ERA and specifically to grasp their interactions, was destined to be complex and challenging. In this section we address some of the methodological issues arising in our own and others' attempts to take up this challenge. We draw particular attention to the connections between our theoretical and conceptual foci and the methodology employed in our research.

As indicated above, our interests in the development of the NCPE encompassed both policy and practice, and were directed towards gaining a greater understanding of why *both* took the *particular* form that they did. Our concern, essentially, was to explore and analyse the processes of the development of a National Curriculum and therefore to investigate the many sites involved in policy making and implementation, the roles of the different sites and the relationships between them. We share Hargreaves' view that education policy research needs to address not either macro or micro aspects of policy, but both of these and what lies between them. It needs to address the 'meso' or middle structures, and to therefore seek to uncover the 'range of intermediary processes and structures which have been largely neglected in sociological accounts of education' (1986: 170). In essence, the need is for a multi-level analysis to capture the ongoing mediation of policy arising from 'local' interpretations and influences (see also Gerwitz *et al.* 1995).

In addition (following Hill 1980), we accept the need for research to address the interaction between policies and point to the significance of this dimension of the policy process in shaping developments in schools. In our own research this meant moving beyond an investigation of 'only' the NCPE to explore instead its development in the context of the 'ERA as a whole' and in relation to the wider social, cultural, political and economic conditions in which it was made and implemented. Our discussion in subsequent chapters illustrates the way in which the interactions between policies, and between policies and the broader contexts in which they are set, are complex and highly significant characteristics in policy and curriculum development in education.

These features of our research point to the dynamic relationship between its theoretical and methodological dimensions; that is, between our view of **policy as a process** (see Chapter 2) and the research design that we regarded as appropriate and necessary to gain a greater understanding of the policies and practices of physical education. Both the theoretical and methodological dimensions of our work were then reflected in, and also informed by, its empirical scope and focus. Relationships between the different dimensions of our work were thus dynamic in nature. Theoretical and methodological concerns informed our choice of sites and methods of data collection, while the emerging data actively informed both our developing theoretical ideas and the research design (in relation to the sites and issues to subsequently focus on and the methods to employ to pursue these). This flexibility is particularly important in research that is addressing contemporary and emerging policies and practices. Essentially, the research has to be able to respond to and keep pace with developments. Consequently, the design cannot be neat and predetermined. We can say with certainty that such research will seem uncomfortably uncertain, very demanding and at times 'messy'. Our research has highlighted that while it may seem logical to investigate different sites sequentially, if we are to gain an understanding of the role and influence of all sites throughout the process, the research (at least to some extent) we need to keep track of developments in *all* sites at *all* times. In short, if research is to promote a greater understanding of the complex nature of policy making and implementation, it needs to embrace that complexity and, therefore, cannot be overly restricted or predetermined in its focus and scope.

A related commitment in this approach to research is an emphasis upon **reflexivity**, involving the ongoing questioning of decisions concerning the focus of the study, what issues are to be pursued and identified and how data gathered are to be used to inform subsequent inquiry. As well as demanding critique of theoretical concepts and data, reflexivity also requires the investigation of the researchers' personal interests and agendas. We have therefore acknowledged the influence of our own established professional and personal interests in education and the agendas that we have sought to pursue in our work (see Evans and Penney 1992; Penney 1994). As we discuss further below (see pp. 14–15), a particular concern was to pursue equality and equity in physical education and to examine whether the policies of central government were advancing the NCPE in the direction of 'PE for all'.

While we were not of the opinion that theorising and documenting changes in educational activity in schools and the interplay of policy forces could or would provide solutions to educational problems in a direct and simplistic way, we none the less began the study committed to try to engage with the policy process. Perhaps naively we hoped that our research would in some small and modest way help to open and extend debate on these issues within physical education and have some impact on future policy and practice. To a degree we therefore saw ours as research not only 'of' but also 'for' policy (Ball 1997). We experienced some disappointment at the apparently limited influence that the study had on emerging developments in physical education in the United Kingdom. However, this apparent failure of research to inform policy seems a common phenomenon in educational research in the UK (see Finch 1986; Hammersley 1994). Whether the lack of influence is an inherent fault of policy research or a reflection of central government's or policy makers' negative attitudes towards it, or their sometimes blunt unwillingness to consider seriously its findings (Kay 1998), is a matter for debate. The latter possibility seems regrettably underplayed in Hammersley's (1994) analysis of the strengths and weaknesses of policy research.

We also need to critically examine how realistic researchers' expectations are, and the best strategies for achieving influence in the policy process. Finch (1986) has usefully drawn attention to the fundamental link between the perceived failure of research findings to be reflected in policy developments and the way in which policy is conceptualised. If, as we discuss further in Chapter 2, we shift from views of policy as a commodity or 'thing' to policy as a complex process, and acknowledge the many interrelated factors that are influential in decisions concerning policy, we can appreciate that the potential input from research will always be limited, but not insignificant. The reality is that 'the practical wisdom generated by research is one factor in educational decisions. Political ideologies, practical constraints, personal and irrational preferences are all influential and currently more so than practical wisdom' (Brown 1991: 10). In the UK we have seen that the impact of research will ultimately be dependent on the willingness of those involved in the policy process to listen and that if research findings and recommendations do not connect with established agendas and political ideologies, then there is little prospect of influence. As Hammersley noted, research on the ERA has typified this problem: 'educational research played little or no role in shaping the act' and furthermore, 'in many respects the legislation goes in opposite directions to those indicated by its [research] findings' (1994: 139).

However, while research may rarely be the critical source of 'enlightenment' that some wish it to be, we should not dismiss all potential for research to play a part in shaping education policies and practice. Conceptualisations of policy may help us to appreciate not only the limitations to the likely influences of research, but also the potential to develop this influence. If as we and others claim, policy making is complex and diffuse, involving many sites and individuals, then researchers need to adopt an approach that actively seeks to infiltrate and permeate the complex structure. We share Finch's view that educational researchers need to broaden out from an interest in influencing those who are regarded as 'makers' of policy, to consider the usefulness of their research to 'other groups who may be in a position to modify policy, albeit in a more limited way, in their day-to-day practice and to groups who are affected by decisions made elsewhere, and have an interest in pressing for change' (Finch 1986: 175). We also support Finch's claim that there is a need to seek to 'inform rather than control the course of change' (ibid.: 176) and that descriptions of situations and experience, rather than 'raw facts' are likely to have a greater potential influence in these terms. Qualitative researchers may not only provide such descriptions but in so doing have the potential to promote a redrawing of the boundaries to problems by formulating and prompting new questions, rather than necessarily providing answers. These were among the aspirations of our own policy research.

Despite our commitment to 'holism' in our research and our emphasis of the need for policy research to embrace the complexities of multiple levels, sites, and policies (see also Ball 1997), like all researchers, we had to acknowledge the limits of our energies and resources. We had no choice but to be selective in our investigations. No researcher, nor research team, can focus upon every dimension of the social world that occupies their interest. In our case, we felt that attempting to embrace both the primary (5–11 years) and secondary (11–16) sectors of education in England and Wales, each a distinct context with important and unique characteristics, would compromise the depth of our investigation and analysis. Consequently, the content of this book reflects the concentrated focus of our research on the secondary sector. While we have less to say on developments concerning primary schools, we nevertheless hope to raise issues that will be of interest to teachers working within that arena. Similarly, although referring in many instances to the study of policies and practices of physical education in England *and* Wales, our investigations hardly begin to address the distinctive developments that have occurred within the latter country. The research upon which this text draws focused primarily on developments in England. Only more recently have we explored the specific developments in Wales, and in so doing have become more aware of how cautious we must be in making generalisations from one cultural context to another. This is equally true when looking at developments *within* each of these countries (see Evans and Davies 1997; Davies, Evans, Penney and Bass 1997). Regional and local differences exist and play an important part in policy developments in both England and Wales. There is a critical local dimension to the policy process, which sees global and national policies and interests taking a particular form and having particular (mediated and contested) influences. This has been evident in our research and we emphasise that not all LEAs, nor all schools and teachers within them responded to the ERA in the ways that we describe in this book. However, this does not detract from the value of our data which none the less illustrate characteristics, trends and complexities of policy development that have variously featured in LEAs and schools throughout England and Wales.

A further shortcoming of our research and writing has been the degree to which certain voices and interests have been represented, while others have been marginalised or excluded. In these respects, policy research is no more neutral than the policies that it seeks to explore and understand. However, again we point to the constraints of our energy and resources and the consequent need for selectivity in our investigations. We did not gather data from all interest groups, and in particular, did not engage with parents or students. Appendix A provides an outline of the scope of our research during the period 1989–1995 and the range of methods that we employed.

Equality and equity: physical education and sport

Inherent in our interest in the development of the National Curriculum for Physical Education in England and Wales were particular views about the purposes of physical education and, critically, who it should be for. We hoped that the development of the NCPE would not only encourage and support moves towards greater equality and equity in the curricula and pedagogies of physical education, but also prompt a radical review of its purposes in respect of the changing conditions and requirements of a post modern world. The extent to which these concerns continue to be marginalised in physical education teaching and teacher education remains a concern. Our data has confirmed that legislating for all children to study a common subject matter does not guarantee that there will be equal opportunity for all to feel valued or to pursue and develop their individual skills and interests. We emphasise that 'equal access' cannot be assumed to provide 'equal opportunity' and that as Byrne (1985) has emphasised, we need to consider 'whether the curriculum to which all have access is just or equitable' (cited in Evans and Davies 1993: 24) and whether the interests of all children are equally acknowledged and addressed in this curriculum. Inherent in this concern for equity is a view of identity and difference as a resource and source of creativity, rather than a problem to be in some way overcome in curriculum design and delivery (ibid.). We therefore take the view that physical education should be concerned with the needs and interests of *all* pupils, and stress that both prior to the ERA and after it, there remain damaging disparities in the resourcing of education, the design of curricula, the teaching methods and grouping strategies used within and between schools. In both physical education and sport, and in educational research, there is a tendency for what Ball (1997) has termed 'golden ageism'; a portrayal that the ERA precipitated all of the shortcomings that we now see in education and physical education. Clearly we need to acknowledge both the strengths and weaknesses of past practice, and also the degree to which historical contexts have had and continue to have a key bearing upon policies and practices in contemporary times.

Finally, there is a need for us to articulate what we regard as a defining characteristic of physical education and, specifically, a characteristic that distinguishes it from sport. Acknowledging that definitions of physical education have changed historically and will differ cross-culturally, we move to a view that the critical and enduring focus in and of physical education is the child or young person. This, in our view, distinguishes physical education from sport. For us sport can be regarded as an important aspect of and vehicle for physical education, but physical education is, and is about, 'more than just sport'. The following chapters vividly illustrate that not all share this view. Before pursuing such debates, however, we turn attention to important underlying conceptualisations central to any analyses of change, reform or development in physical education and education more broadly. Specifically, we address the nature of the relationship between policy and practice in education, and the much talked about gap between them. In Chapter 8 we return to the matters of equality and equity in the context of contemporary developments in physical education in England and Wales and elsewhere.

Summary

The Education Reform Act (ERA) 1988 was the Conservative government's response to a claimed crisis in state education in England and Wales. It comprised a complex package of policies designed to change fundamentally both the content of state education, and the nature and structure of the education system itself. On the one hand, it detailed arrangements for the development of a National Curriculum. This was to comprise studies in core and foundation subjects and would be linked to standardised national testing. Despite being identified as a National Curriculum foundation subject, it was unclear what the future of physical education in schools would be, what would emerge as a National Curriculum for Physical Education and how schools would be variously placed to respond to the new statutory requirements. Via other policies (local management of schools (LMS) and open enrolment, in particular), the ERA established a quasi free market for education, in which schools were given new financial and management responsibilities. Funding for schools became explicitly linked to the intake of pupils, and headteachers and school governing bodies were accorded the tasks of ensuring that they attracted pupils in sufficient numbers for their school to survive and prosper in the new market conditions, and of dividing resources between departments (and competing needs) within their schools.

The ERA was also a catalyst for a great deal of educational research and, particularly, policy research in education. The complexities and political nature of the ERA raised critical challenges for those seeking to document and analyse its effects on curricula, teaching and learning in schools. The complexities of the ERA needed to be reflected in the design of research seeking to make a contribution to understandings of policy in education. Such research needed to maintain a holistic approach, address the many sites involved in policy making and implementation, and take account of the ongoing interactions between policies, and between policies and the broader social, economic, political and historical contexts in which they were set. The research reported in the following chapters attempted to take up these challenges in specifically exploring the development and implementation of the National Curriculum for Physical Education. It sought in particular to pursue not only the complexities of policy and curriculum development in physical education, but also issues of equality and equity in the policies and practices of PE.

Further reading

For further details of the ERA's policies readers should refer to government publications and in particular:

DES (1989a) *National Curriculum – From Policy to Practice*. London: DES.
DES (1988) 'E.R.A.: L.M.S.' *Circular No. 7/88*. London: DES.

as well as commentaries on the ERA and the political backdrop to the act, such as:

Apple, M. W. (1993) *Official Knowledge*. London: Routledge.
Maclure, S. (1989) *Education Re-formed*. London: Hodder & Stoughton.
Simon, B. (1988) *Bending the Rules. The Baker 'Reform' of Education*. London: Lawrence & Wishart Ltd.

In addition, the edited collection *International Perspectives on Educational Reform and Policy Implementation* (Carter and O'Neill 1995, Falmer Press) includes chapters that address comparable developments in the USA, Australia and New Zealand, and that pursue the significance of global, national and local contexts and agendas in contemporary developments in education.

Useful texts addressing policy research include:

Finch, J. (1986) *Research and Policy. The Uses of Qualitative Methods in Social and Educational Research*. London: Falmer Press.
Halpin, D. and Troyna, B. (eds) (1994) *Researching Education Policy. Ethical and Methodological Issues*. London: Falmer Press.

For further discussion of matters of equity and equality in physical education, see

Evans, J. (ed.) (1993) *Equality, Education and Physical Education*. London: Falmer Press.

Chapter 2

Policy matters

'Education policy research' has come of age in recent years, particularly in the United Kingdom. The ERA was the catalyst for the development of a body of research concerned with education policy and such has been the impact of this work that Troyna described the ERA as providing 'the most important shot in the arm to the study of education policy in Britain' (1994: 2). However, the 'label' and the theoretical location of this body of work have remained problematic and much debated issues (see for example Grace 1984; Henry 1993; Lingard 1993; Whitty 1997). In the United Kingdom 'education policy sociology' has been one of the more popular terms adopted for the new and growing body of work. Variously authors have attempted to fill a perceived gap in existing policy literature by taking a new approach to the study of policy within education. The emerging work can be seen as attempting to address what Raab (1994) has argued has been a two-fold neglect in the study of politics and policy in education. On the one hand, Raab sees 'political scientists' and work in 'policy studies' as failing to produce a body of research specifically relating to education and, on the other, he identifies educationalists as rarely focusing their attention on policy matters. Our own research and this book seek to contribute to the new ways of conceptualising policy and the new body of literature within the sociology of education.

Looking at things differently: new thoughts on policy

In what can be regarded as ground-breaking research on education policy in the UK, Stephen Ball (1990b) and his colleagues (Bowe *et al.* 1992; Gerwitz, *et al.* 1995) have highlighted the shortcomings in the 'managerial' and 'bureaucratic' perspectives on policy that historically have dominated research concerned with social and educational administration and organisation (see also Ham and Hill 1984). Equally, we can reflect that these perspectives have not only been confined to research environments, but have also been expressed in the professional activity and structures of many organisations. Thus in both research and in the workings of organisations, policy and practice have tended to be portrayed as quite distinct phenomena. Policy is reified as an artefact, commodity or 'thing', made by certain individuals usually in the upper echelons of organisations, systems or the state, to be implemented by others in levels or sites 'below', thereby giving rise to 'practice'. The relationship is clearly hierarchical. In this conceptualisation policy and practice are emphasised as different and distinct, as are policy 'making' and 'implementation'. The dominant direction of the relationship between these two phenomena is downward. In the context of education, agencies and individuals associated with central government are emphasised as having a *determining* influence of over what happens in schools. Teachers are seen as the last, and least important, link in the chain of decision making; the subjects of, and for, the whims of powerful others outside schools, occupying positions in central government or other agencies of the state. Implicit in this conceptualisation is also a particular view of knowledge, as something that is and can be pre-determined and identified, and duly 'delivered' to children in schools (see also Taylor, Rizvi, Lingard and Henry 1997).

Influenced by this 'traditional' conceptualisation of policy, much of the policy studies research in education has served to reinforce rather than challenge views about policy and, in particular, the common distinction and divide between the arenas of 'policy' and 'practice' (Bowe *et al.* 1992). Bowe *et al.* explain that many studies have been concerned with the actions of central government (or other agencies of the state) and have examined policy statements and documents produced at this level, while, in parallel, others have developed work focusing on implementation and centring attention on schools and teachers within them. The former studies (see for example Dudley and Vidovich 1995; Graham with Tytler 1993) have productively identified the interests and biases in the agendas of decision makers at sites of decision making outside schools (particularly governments and their aides) and the 'authority' ascribed to the texts and statements forthcoming from these sites. The latter (see for example Hoyle 1986; Sabatier 1993) have promoted a 'bottom-up' view of the policy–practice relationship, emphasising the active role of the practitioner in the development of policy and curriculum change and the degree to which many policies in education are influenced and shaped by what happens in schools. The contribution of both approaches is certainly important, as they have addressed quite different directions of influence in relation to policy. However, at the same time both have left the distinction between policy and practice and between policy makers and practitioners, essentially unchallenged. Reflecting upon the contribution of 'implementation studies' to policy analysis, Ham and Hill noted that:

Its very strength in stressing the importance of the implementation process as distinguishable from the policy-making process, and deserving of study in its own right, has tended to lead to the weakness of overemphasising the distinctiveness of the two processes. There has been a tendency to treat policies as clear cut, uncontroversial entities, whose implementation can be quite separately studied.

(1984: 95)

Below we expand upon what we regard as critical shortcomings of the 'traditional' distinctions in conceptualising policy and outline the notably different view of policy that has informed our own and others' research concerned with contemporary developments in education. In Troyna's view this recent work has had 'a healthy disregard for managerialist and bureaucratic conceptions of the policy process' (1994: 4). It has drawn on a variety of theoretical and disciplinary sources to help complexify our view of policy and make sense of what has occurred in education in recent years. Specifically, studies in education policy sociology have variously sought to gain a better understanding of the relationship between policy statements issued by identified 'makers' of policy and the often contradictory, contrasting and unintended practices subsequently arising in schools. At the same time, this work has also endeavoured to explore how research can actively inform and influence both policy and practice in education. Although education policy sociology is still a new and developing field, with 'uncertain theoretical grounding' (Raab 1994), in our view the 'experimentalism' of the work undertaken has breathed new life into research within the sociology of education and has presented the potential for further exploration and development, and particularly so in the sociology of physical education. Like Ball (1997) we see the value of developing an interplay of theories while at the same time carefully retaining coherency in our work.

Policy as a process

As indicated above, work grounded in managerialist and bureaucratic conceptualisations of policy has tended to adopt either a 'macro' or 'micro' focus, centring respectively on the 'generation' or 'implementation' of policy. The former focus has been concerned with the structures of, for example, the state or central government, overlying and surrounding schools; the latter with the schools themselves, departments and individuals within them. Deconstructing the divide between policy and practice and attempting to bridge the 'gap' between macro and micro analyses have been key characteristics of work in education policy sociology. This work has been particularly concerned to develop a more holistic view of policy as a complex process, embracing what have previously been termed 'generation' and 'implementation' perspectives and specifically seeking to explore the relationships between different sites of decision making and action. It therefore regards, explores and portrays policy 'as process and not merely substance' (Raab 1994: 24).

This way of thinking about policy assumes that neither making nor implementation is confined to a single site, nor particular individuals, nor a specific moment in time. As we illustrate in the chapters that follow, adaptation, modification and contestation of policy can occur at various points in what is typically termed implementation, as policy is continually made and remade at sites throughout the process, though rarely, we stress, in conditions that are without constraint, or that are not framed by the actions, discursive practices and policy decisions of others. None the less it becomes abundantly clear that the conceptual isolation of policy making from implementation obfuscates or worse still, denies, the creative dimensions of the latter, and also, the complexity and number of influences and individuals that variously play a part in policy making. In later chapters we illustrate both the influences but also the restrictions on the roles of different individuals in the policy process. First, we explore further some concepts that are central to the analysis and understanding of this creativity, constraint and complexity in relation to policy.

Multiple sites; multiple texts

Inherent in a view of policy as a process is the recognition of the need to understand the links between the 'macro' and 'micro' levels of action and decision making; to investigate both levels, but also (and particularly if we are to gain a better understanding of the frequently reported gap between policy and practice) the nature of the relationships between them. In addressing this relationship we see that there are not only two levels to the process, but rather many, often overlapping sites of action. For example, communication between politicians and teachers in schools is rarely direct. It may involve many people located in many different sites of practice. Exploration of the links and relationships between the 'macro' and the 'micro' contexts highlights the influence of mediating organisations and individuals *between* these levels and the need therefore, for policy analyses to also embrace these influences and sites. Hargreaves (1986) has emphasised that these 'intermediary' sites at what he terms a 'meso' level are influential in shaping both the 'policies' that subsequent sites receive and also the economic, political and ideological contexts in which policies will be interpreted. In Reynolds' view, the failure to address these influences has been a key shortcoming of previous studies within the sociology of education. He explains:

When the sociology of education has looked at practice, it has usually
looked at classrooms, not at the schools, the LEAs or other educational sectors that are most involved in framing policy changes.

(1989: 191)

Reynold's comments clearly direct us to examine the education system *as
a whole* in considering the making and implementation of policy, even
though his later work on effectiveness in schools often seems to abandon
this worthy sociological ideal (see Whitty 1997). Ball has similarly stressed
the need for policy research to adopt what he terms a 'trajectory perspective' that 'attends to the ways in which policies evolve, change and decay
through time and space and their coherence' (1997: 266). What such an
approach acknowledges is that the making and implementation of policy
involves a series of communications within and between various sites of
educational systems, with policy 'transmitted', and as we explain further
below, *transformed* in this process.

Hill (1980) was led to conceptualise the policy process as a 'chain
image' with sites or individuals being 'links' and the process comprising
a series of links. In education we can see central government departments,
local government, senior school staff, heads of departments and teachers
as such 'links'. In subsequent chapters we explore the role that each of
these played in the development of the National Curriculum for Physical
Education (NCPE) in England and Wales and in so doing highlight other
important characteristics of the policy process. Most notably, we emphasise that policy making and implementation involve the transmission of
not one, but rather a series of different policy texts. This dimension
of the policy process has been a key focus of Ball and his colleagues'
recent research and writings on education policy (see Bowe *et al.* 1992).
Bowe *et al.* have stressed that whenever a policy is received, it will be
read and interpreted in this process, and a 'new' or 'hybrid' text will then
be produced by the reader. Inevitably and unavoidably therefore, there
will be 'slippage' in the policy process (ibid.). Policy, its emphases and
meanings, will change to a greater or lesser degree in this process. Each
reading of a policy will differ to some degree; all individuals have their
own interpretation and understanding of a text. As a result, the text subsequently communicated to others may be quite different to that 'received'
by those now communicating its content, intent and/or application.
However, while recognising this ongoing potential for change in relation
to policy, it is also important to note similarities and continuities that run
throughout the process, and to recognise that aspects of policies remain
unchanged and/or unchallenged. Understanding and exploring both the
changes and continuities in the policy process demands that we take a
closer look at the nature of texts, what is involved in their production
and transmission, and the matters of who has the 'authority' and 'power'

(see Chapter 7) to determine agendas and to decide what is worthwhile knowledge in education.

So what is a policy text?

Firstly we need to emphasise that in talking of texts we are not only referring to written (re-)conceptualisations of policy. Rather, a text may take a written, spoken, mental or corporeal form, and the latter may of course, have particular significance in physical education (see Shilling 1993). In reading any written text or listening to a spoken text, we produce our own 'mental map' of that text, and it is that mental map rather than the 'original' text that will be our reference point in responding to policy (Penney 1994). We each produce our own texts, formal and visible, or not. In education systems it is often the case that individuals are required to respond to a policy by producing a further document or statement addressing the policy and its implications at a more local level. For example, historically in England and Wales, Local Education Authorities (LEAs) have each produced their own responses to central government initiatives. Invariably it is the LEA policy, rather than the central government's text, that schools within that authority will 'act upon'. However, in acting upon this policy, once again there will be interpretation and what Bernstein (1996) calls 'recontextualisation' of policy, and thus the creation of a 'new' or 'hybrid' text. The LEA policy is interpreted and may be adapted in various ways within schools, and departments within them. The process of interpretation and re-creation of texts is thus ongoing and can be regarded as constituting a 'flow' of policy between sites and individuals (Penney 1994). Ultimately texts are embodied and enacted corporeally in schools and classrooms, and as teachers and pupils interact, modify and shape their readings of (texts and) each other within the idiosyncratic conditions of their work. However, while we can now see the multiplicity of texts, we have no greater insight into what makes them different. To understand this, we need to address the concept of **discourse**.

Unpacking texts

The concept of discourse, now widely but often inconsistently used in sociological and educational research (see Luke 1995) enables us to examine the values and interests that texts express and promote, and the alternatives that they overlook, marginalise or exclude. Of central concern in theories of discourse are 'language and meaning', matters that 'have often been taken for granted in policy analysis in the past' (Taylor 1997: 25). Our own use of the term, to a degree influenced by post-structural social theory and in particular by the analyses of contemporary culture by Michel Foucault (1972, 1977, 1980), emphasises the:

constructing character of discourse, that is how, both in broader social formations (i.e., epistemes) and in local sites and uses discourse actually defines, constructs and positions human subjects. According to Foucault (1972, p. 49) discourses 'systemically form the objects about which they speak', shaping grids and hierarchies for the institutional categorisation and treatment of people.

(Luke 1995: 8)

In this view discourse is not only about what is said, but also what is *not* said. Ball's Foucauldian usage of the term, explains 'discourses construct certain possibilities for thought. They order and combine words in particular ways and exclude or displace other combinations' (1990b: 18). Discourses are expressions of particular interests and values, they create and promote particular meanings and values. We see that texts:

... include what is not written as well as what is written ... Texts include traces of words and concepts not present, and that which is not present makes possible that which is present.

(Cherryholms 1988, cited in Sparkes 1992: 273)

Critically no text is neutral, but rather all texts have a particular form and content, inherent in which are particular interests and ideologies. Any text will include and privilege certain interests and ideologies, and equally, subordinate or exclude others. Inevitably, texts are political, serving and promoting, but equally overlooking and subordinating, particular interests.

The concept of discourse is thus a key tool in our exploration and understanding of policies. It helps us to investigate not only the origins of policies in broader social formations (for example in capitalism and the formations of social class and patriarchy, see Apple 1993) and 'regimes of truth', but also the particular form that policies have at particular points in time and in different sites in the policy process. Exploration of discourses in relation to policy thus enables us to describe changes in policy throughout their development and progression through education systems. In the process of 'slippage' (Bowe *et al.* 1992) (the interpretation, adaptation, adoption and modification of policy) we see contestation and struggle over discourses, reinforcement and/or rejection of discourses present in the texts and, potentially, the introduction of new discourses to those texts. In the following chapters we illustrate this contestation very vividly in tracking and analysing the development of the National Curriculum for Physical Education in England and Wales.

A further important point for us to note here is that all texts contain **multiple discourses**, some of which will be privileged over others. It is inappropriate to talk of a policy document expressing 'an' or 'the' official discourse of a government or organisation. As we will see, the complexity of the policy process is such that texts always and inevitably represent and contain various discourses. Differences in the relative visibility of particular discourses, the privileging of some over others, is central to the notion of slippage in the implementation of policy. If we are to understand the particular form that texts take we need not only to look closely at the texts themselves, but also to address other complexities of the policy process. Of primary concern here is that policies do not exist in isolation. Rather they arise from, and throughout the process enter and interact with, specific contexts (with particular economic, political, social and ideological characteristics). In this process texts also act, themselves, to shape those contexts in particular ways. There is thus a critical dynamic in the policy process. Policy 'content' is both shaped by and shapes the contexts in which policies are made and implemented. Returning to our discussion of discourses, what we emphasise here is that contexts as well as texts contain multiple discourses, privileging some, and subordinating and omitting others. Like other analysts of education policy (Apple 1982, 1993) we stress the significance of the discourses 'surrounding' texts; that is, those featuring in the contexts of their development and reading, and impacting upon those developments and readings. Like Taylor (1997) we therefore stress the value of the concept of discourse not only for explorations of policy texts, but also of the discursive fields within which texts arise and are responded to.

In subsequent chapters we show how discourses dominant in wider contexts of educational and political arenas, for example of competitive individualism and cultural restoration, shaped interpretations of and responses to the texts of the National Curriculum for Physical Education in England and Wales. In this respect we see evidence of not only national but also global social, economic and ideological influences. Again, however, we stress that the influences are two-way. We identify the discourses within the texts of the NCPE as actively shaping contexts of policy making and implementation and draw attention to the ways in which texts served to either reinforce or challenge the dominance of particular discourses, and thereby helped to create particular possibilities for thoughts and actions in the policy process. Following Hill (1980) and more recently Taylor *et al.* (1997) and Ball (1997) we also stress the interaction **between different policies.** Hill explained that 'There is a cumulative process to be analysed in which policies create needs for other policies, opportunities for other policies, and new social situations for further political responses' (1980: 11), and that policies are 'to a considerable extent products of other policies' (ibid.). In addition, he stressed that 'Even policies with little direct impact upon each other will be "rivals" for scarce resources' (ibid.: 106) and problems and incompatibilities in the process may give rise not only to inter-policy but also inter-agency issues.

Who has what say?

In addressing the dynamic between texts and contexts we hit upon one of the many problematic issues in policy analyses; the blurred boundary between the 'content' and 'contexts' of the policy process. This 'blurring' becomes most obvious when considering another important feature of the process; the **arrangements for policy** (Hill 1980). Hill identified the arrangements for policy development and implementation as often an explicit and integral part of policies, but also as critical in creating particular conditions that shape their development and subsequent expression. Throughout the following chapters we illustrate the way in which particular arrangements for policy established in and by the ERA were critical in shaping the development of the National Curriculum in England and Wales. In so doing, we also confront an aspect of the policy process that has to this point been overlooked in our discussion; the matter of **inequality** in relation to policy. In this respect we address a shortcoming that Hill (1980) himself identified in the chain image of policy making and implementation; that although more complex than some 'top-down' models, the chain still portrays the policy process as linear and somewhat 'automatic' in terms of the links involved. That is to say, it is implied that policy flows freely around and through the links, and that there is equality among and between the individuals or agencies in the chain. In reality however, 'varying responsibilities and degrees of autonomy are involved, and individuals in the chain may be bypassed' (Hill 1980: 83). Different sizes of link would go some way towards depicting an element of the inequality in relation to the relative influence that different individuals and sites have in the policy process, but this too fails to acknowledge the capacity for policy sites and/or individuals to be overlooked or bypassed in the process. Taylor *et al.* draw attention to such inequalities, saying that 'Not all influence this process equally; often there is conflict and contradiction between the perspectives and interests of those involved, and not all players benefit equally' (1997: 15). In our investigation of the development of the NCPE in England and Wales we clearly see inequalities in influence and 'authority' in relation to the scope and potential for particular individuals to speak and be heard in the policy process and, furthermore, for different interests and discourses to be included, excluded, privileged and/or subordinated. We see that discourses are 'about what can be said, and thought, but also about "*who can speak where, when and with what authority*"' (Ball 1990b: 17, our emphasis) and that the arrangements for policy have a critical influence in relation to these matters.

It is not a one-way track

While emphasising important aspects of complexity and inequality, we have been guilty in our discussion thus far of portraying the process as only one-way. A shortcoming that we see in Hill's chain image is the tendency to portray the flow of policy as unidirectional; downward from central government via local government to schools, and then from senior administrative staff to heads of departments and individual teachers. Undoubtedly the policy process in education involves at least a two-way flow of text and discourse within and between sites. There are mechanisms whereby sites play an active role in the policy making and implementation of sites 'above' them and there are a complexity of relations between various sites. Thus we need to view the process as involving multiple flows (Penney 1994). In subsequent chapters we illustrate and analyse the potential for 'upward' flow in the policy process and the complexity of interactions between sites. However, we also stress the inequalities in influence inherent in these interactions. Perhaps somewhat ironically, in studying the progressive development of the National Curriculum for Physical Education in England and Wales, we have been led to emphasise the limits and constraints of the 'upward flow' and to highlight in particular the *determining* influence of central government *throughout* the process. Consequently we have emphasised the need for caution in making assumptions about the capacity for slippage in relation to policy. Increasingly we have sought to develop a framework for our analyses that accommodates the complexities of the process that we have identified above and yet, at the same time, also articulates and makes explicit what we regard as an important, if subtle, linear dimension to the process. Inherent in this linear dimension, certainly in the case of the policies that we have explored, has been an important element of central government 'control' in and of the process, with visibly limited capacities for others in that process to pursue *different* interests and agendas. In our work we have consequently been seeking a framework that in particular addresses the matters of 'power', 'agency' and 'control' in relation to policy and curriculum development and, to date, one of the most useful concepts that we have employed is that of 'frame'.

This concept is drawn from the work of Bernstein (1971, 1990, 1996) and Lundgren (1977) which attempted to articulate the conceptual link 'between teaching and levels above teaching' (Lundgren 1977: 82), to identify factors that limited teachers' freedom to develop different pedagogies, and register the strength of constraints and/or or possibilities in teaching and curriculum development. Critically the concept of frame prompts us to explore 'who controls what' in pedagogical and policy processes. It has been central to our attempts to articulate the relational balance between human agency and structure (matters that we return to in Chapter 7) and in particular, the 'freedom' and 'control' experienced by individuals and agencies at various policy sites; the potential for, but also 'boundaries' to, the slippage possible in the policy process. Essentially we have seen the actions of individuals at various policy sites being both restricted and to a degree directed by a complex range of factors, but, particularly, by preceding events in the policy process. The view that we have developed is of the process involving the progressive creation of frames or boundaries within which slippage is possible, but also clearly limited. Our data suggest that while the policy process often involves the production of multiple texts, there are both differences and similarities in these texts. Thus there is the capacity not only for change but also for important elements of continuity and control in the making and implementation of policy. In exploring the aspects and underpinnings of this control we have also noted that our own use and conceptualisation of frame has differed from Lundgren's. Lundgren (1977) distinguished between factors 'constraining' and factors 'governing' the teaching process, and used frame only in relation to the former. However, our data suggest that 'governing' factors should equally be regarded as constituting a constraint in the policy process and should therefore be seen as a frame in that process. In our discussion of the development of the National Curriculum for Physical Education in England and Wales we show that while there were certainly struggles between discourses and changes in their relative status, there were also notable continuities in the discourses included and privileged in texts. The concept of frame has been central to our investigation of who and what has underpinned, facilitated and encouraged continuity in and control of the policy process, and, in particular, set the boundaries to what could and would be considered as an appropriate National Curriculum for Physical Education. We have identified frames arising from both the content of policy and the contexts of development and implementation, and have attempted to distinguish between different types of frame operating in the process. Here we present what we stress are provisional thoughts about categories of frames in the policy process, in an effort to articulate the range of different factors that may give rise to barriers and boundaries to thoughts and actions in policy development.

Framing policy

Above we indicated our interest in discourses and specifically, the way in which texts include, exclude, privilege and/or subordinate particular discursive orientations. As we will see, negotiation over the form and content of the National Curriculum for Physical Education followed increasingly narrow agendas and saw a clear privileging of particular interests and discourses, and the parallel subordination of others. What we describe in the chapters that follow is the creation and progressive reinforcement of particular 'discursive frames' in the policy process (Penney 1994) which themselves originate from a combination of neo-liberal and conservative 'truths' about the needs of the individual, industry and social order within civil society and the state (see also Apple 1993; Kay 1998). In addressing the nature and strength of these discourses we draw heavily on the inspirational work of Bernstein (1971, 1990, 1996) that has explored the form, content and message systems of school curricula. In Chapter 3 we introduce and apply concepts developed by Bernstein to explore the structure and inherent values of the National Curriculum for Physical Education, and to interrogate the nature and degree of 'power', 'control' and 'direction' inherent in the discursive dimension of policy. However, in pursuing these interests we also see very clearly that 'the power of one discourse to prevail over another does not depend solely on *discursive* power, but can draw upon institutional, positional and material forms of power also' (Maw 1993: 58). Theorising policy thus means also addressing **structural** issues relating to policy and identifying, specifically, the characteristics of structural constraints and their implications for the discursive freedoms enjoyed by individuals or agencies in the policy process. We highlight that extant policy and social structures can themselves comprise frames that position individuals and their respective interests in certain ways and restrict their freedom in the policy process. New policies do not enter terrains that are a policy *tabula rasa*, but rather contexts that are already conditioned and framed by the struggles, actions and decision making of those that have gone before. We also stress that **political, ideological** and **economic** influences bear heavily on policy (see Apple 1982, 1993; Gerwitz *et al.* 1995; Lingard 1993; Taylor *et al.* 1997) and we identify these as further types or sources of frame. In later chapters we illustrate the ways in which the development of the National Curriculum was directed and constrained by the political and ideological agendas of the Conservative New Right, set in and limited by contexts of economic constraint. We also highlight important links between various frames arising in the policy process. In particular we identify economic and political frames as generating particular discursive frames. Once again, therefore, we emphasise complexity in relation to policy and the difficulty of any conceptual framework to clearly and adequately embrace this. In Chapter 7 we return to this problem, reflecting upon our empirical illustration of the many subtleties of policy. We now turn our attention to the illustration and seek to show the relevance and application of the concepts that we have discussed here.

Summary

The ERA has been a catalyst for a body of work within the sociology of education that has sought to explore and promote new conceptualisations of policy. In particular, this work has challenged the view that policy making and implementation are separate and distinct activities, each confined to specific sites and/or individuals. The emphasis has been upon seeing policy as an ongoing and highly complex process, involving the production of and contestation over many texts. All texts will express, promote, subordinate or exclude particular interests and the concept of discourse is central in understanding this characteristic of texts. All texts contain multiple discourses that will be variously privileged or subordinated throughout the progressive development of policies. There is also the capacity for new discourses to be embedded in texts as the policy process progresses. However, not everyone has an equal say in determining the inclusion and/or visibility of particular discourses. In attempting to understand what underpins the particular form of texts, we also need to address who has what say in relation to policy and how policies interact with each other, and with wider social, economic, political and ideological contexts and agendas. The challenge in theorising policy is to develop a framework that captures the complexity of influences and in particular that can portray notions of control and direction as well as freedom and creativity in the policy process. A concept that may be useful in this respect is that of frame. It is suggested that a variety of influences (discursive, structural, economic, political) variously 'frame' the ongoing development of policy, and that frames interact in complex ways to limit the thinking and actions of those involved in making and implementing policies in education.

Further reading

Bowe, R. and Ball, S.J. with Gold, A. (1992) *Reforming Education and Changing Schools*. London: Routledge.

provides further commentary on the background to the development of new sociological studies centring on education policy.

Apple's work is particularly useful in exploring the location of policy developments in wider social, economic and political contexts and thus also addressing global dimensions to policy developments in education. See:

Apple, M.W. (1982) *Education and Power*. London: Ark.
Apple, M.W. (1993) *Official Knowledge*. London: Routledge.

Other general policy texts that have stood the test of time include:

Hill, M. (1980) *Understanding Social Policy*. Oxford: Basil Blackwell.
Ham, C. and Hill, M. (1984) *The Policy Process in the Modern Capitalist State*. London: Wheatsheaf Books Ltd.

In addition, our discussion in Chapter 3 points to the significance of Bernstein's work in analyses of the particular form of curricula and their implications. Finally, in Chapter 7 we introduce texts that are useful in pursuing the concepts of power, authority, structure and agency in relation to policy.

Chapter 3

Politics and policy: making a National Curriculum for Physical Education

In Chapter 1 we outlined the context in which our research arose and explained the package of policies that constituted the Education Reform Act (ERA). In Chapter 2 we reinforced the need, in analysing the production of particular texts, to address the context of their development and to understand the interactions between different policies. In now focusing on the development of the National Curriculum for Physical Education (NCPE) in England and Wales we therefore begin by reminding readers of the other policies incorporated in the ERA and the particular economic and political interests that were set to impact upon the NCPE.

Responding to the 'crisis' in education

According to New Right politicians (many ill disposed to let the evidence from educational research obstruct their ideological beliefs; see Simon 1988) comprehensive schools and child-centred progressivism within them, had miserably failed Britain's youth, delivering neither the form nor the content of education that pupils and their prospective employers required. In the rhetoric of New Right thinking it was time to return to 'basics', restore 'traditional' teaching methods, break the hold that teachers and Local Education Authorities (LEAs) held on curriculum matters, and elevate the interests of consumers (parents and pupils) in the education process. It was claimed that these measures would raise standards in education and indeed, were required to achieve this. However, central government was operating in an economic and political climate in which there were neither the resources to invest in developments in education or other public services, nor the political desire to do so. The package of policies that constituted the ERA thus both reflected and cleverly sought to resolve this tension faced by the government. The introduction of local management of schools (LMS) signalled a clear shift in responsibility for the provision of education to individual schools and answered calls for greater efficiency in education. Meanwhile, the introduction of the National Curriculum and its accompanying requirements for assessment and reporting provided clear accountability in education and could be seen as directly addressing the concerns for 'improved standards' in schools. Thus, in a context that emphasised new 'freedom' for schools operating in an education market, the ERA presented the opportunity for increased central government control of the curriculum. Notably, however, responsibility for the successful implementation and delivery of the curriculum lay very clearly with LEAs, schools and the teachers within them. The government explained that LEAs and their inspectors and advisers (see Chapter 5) would 'have a key role in preparing for implementation', specifically 'supporting schools in their planning' and providing in-service training for teachers (DES 1989a, 9.10). Meanwhile it was anticipated that headteachers and teachers would address 'the organisation of the curriculum and the scope and content of schemes of work, as well as arranging to take part in relevant INSET [in-service education of teachers]' (ibid., 9.11). It was openly acknowledged that 'The commitment of individual teachers will be crucial in "making it happen"' (ibid., 9.15). Teachers and LEAs, were therefore cleverly (re-)positioned in the policy process. They would not be the makers of the curriculum, but would be vital cogs in the wheels of its delivery.

The National Curriculum: neither new nor neutral

In addressing the claimed 'crisis' in education, the National Curriculum did not propose a new or creative framework for school curricula. Rather, it sought to 're-establish' a 'traditional' and easily recognisable curriculum in all state schools in England and Wales, centring on traditional subjects (maths, English, history, geography, etc.) and reinforcing long-standing hierarchies between them. The National Curriculum bore what has been described as an 'uncanny resemblance' to the curriculum set down in the Secondary School Regulations of 1904, i.e. 'the curriculum of the publicly funded grammar schools established under the Education Act of 1902' (Aldrich 1995; Goodson 1993). The possibility of a curriculum with a very different structure and focus (for example, a thematic based curriculum) received some mention early in discussions, but this idea was soon dispelled in the development of the National Curriculum. There was recognition that the 'whole curriculum' needed to address cross-curricular matters as well as subject-based material (DES 1989a; NCC 1990) but never any serious consideration that such matters could be the *primary* focus for structuring and planning the curriculum. Adopting a structure with the attainment targets and programmes of study (see Chapter 1) centring on themes (for example, personal and social development) rather than traditional subjects, would have promoted a more 'integrated' (Bernstein 1971, 1990, 1996) view of knowledge, and potentially also redefined what was educationally worth while. Significantly, however, such a curriculum would not have been as easy for government ministers to grasp. Lawton has explained that:

> the national curriculum content was expressed in a very conventional way indeed – a list of subjects that any MP [Member of Parliament] would immediately recognise and regard as 'sound common-sense'. The HMI [Her Majesty's Inspectorate] Entitlement Model (based on 'Areas of Experience' rather than subjects) was ignored. It was unfamiliar and looked suspiciously like 'educational theory' – an increasingly taboo concept.
>
> (1993: 65, emphasis removed)

Thus we begin to appreciate that there is little that is arbitrary or accidental about the content of the curriculum in schools. Historically and contemporaneously curricula have comprised a selection from culture, a packaging of what is thought at given times and in given places, to be educationally and socially desirable and worth while. As such, curricula are neither apolitical nor value free. In Bernstein's (1990, 1996) terms schools portray certain categories (or 'specialised contexts') of knowledge as legitimate or valid, and the texts that we produce (as educationalists of one sort or another) both arise from and serve to reinforce or potentially challenge these categories and the boundaries between them. For Bernstein **recognition rules** are the key to distinguishing between specialised contexts of knowledge and so recognising the speciality that constitutes a context. He explains that it is the relationships (and boundaries) between contexts that are the key factor in their legitimation and maintenance. The **principle of classification** defines these categories and shapes the contents and relationships arising from them and the strength of classification determines the degree of specialisation of (and insulation between) categories. The categories thus have a particular identity, or 'voice' and how we then express this voice (and thus develop what we now recognise as a legitimate context of knowledge) is, according to Bernstein, determined by **realisation rules**. However, the realised form of the voice (that Bernstein terms the 'message') has, in Bernstein's view, the capacity to either reinforce or challenge the voice (identity and categorisation of knowledge). Thus while our texts arise within the specific contexts defined by the voice, they can themselves either reinforce the boundaries between different contexts, or challenge them.

This is complex, but valuable in our analyses of curriculum structures. We can see that the structure for curricula define what constitute specific contexts and identities within them. In the case of the National Curriculum for England and Wales, these centred upon traditional subjects. Development of the curriculum content was to occur within these defined fields. In Bernstein's terms, the curriculum was strongly classified; that is, subjects (and consequently the people within them) were positioned as quite distinct from one another. Similarities between them, points of overlap, integration and mutuality, were all a secondary concern. Instead, the distinction between subjects and the unique contribution that each could make to the 'whole curriculum' was emphasised. Developments in physical education, or indeed any of the National Curriculum subjects, then had the potential to reaffirm and reinforce these boundaries between different fields of knowledge, or, equally, could reduce the insulation between them and, in so doing, challenge the principle of classification itself. Throughout this and subsequent chapters we therefore reflect on the development of the National Curriculum for Physical Education in relation to first, how it was shaped or framed by this overlying principle of classification for the curriculum as a whole, and also, whether the texts and practices developed in physical education reinforced or challenged the principle. As indicated in Chapter 2, key concepts to employ in this analysis are those of discourse and discursive frames.

A second rate subject

As well as privileging subject-based knowledge, the National Curriculum clearly emphasised some subjects over and above others. As explained in Chapter 1 it distinguished between 'core' (English, mathematics, science and in Welsh-speaking schools in Wales, Welsh) and 'foundation' (technology, history, geography, modern foreign language, art, music, physical education and in non-Welsh-speaking schools in Wales, Welsh) subjects. Clear priorities both between the core and foundation subjects and *within* the latter, were also explicit in the schedule set for the development and implementation of the National Curriculum. Physical education was among the last subjects to 'come on line' (see Chapter 1). As we will see, the phased pattern of development and implementation and the positioning of physical education late in this process had a notable impact upon both the development of the NCPE and its implementation in schools. In Hill's (1980) terms, this was a key 'arrangement for policy' that remained influential throughout the policy process.

Differences in the status of the various foundation subjects were also evident in the government's comments regarding the scope and depth of the prescriptive requirements for particular subjects. Specifically, it was explained that the extent to which attainment targets and programmes of study would aim to cover the ground in each foundation subject area would vary and that 'For music, art and PE, there are likely to be *very general* national targets' (DES 1989a, 4.16–4.17, our emphasis). In addition it was explained that the attainment targets and programmes of study would 'reflect general assumptions about the amount of time appropriate for the core and other foundation subjects in the curriculum' (ibid., 4.3). The framework for the National Curriculum was clearly not, therefore, one in which all subjects would be equal. Rather, their place and status in the curriculum would reflect the historical and established hierarchy of school subjects in the United Kingdom, and the specific arrangements for the phased development of the National Curriculum reinforced and further legitimated this hierarchy. Given that the curriculum time to be devoted to each of the subjects was not specified, those subjects positioned late in the development process were certainly not in the secure position that their identification as a 'foundation subject' had initially implied.

Specifying the timetable for the development of the National Curriculum subjects was not, however, by any means the only important arrangement for policy development established by the ERA. As explained in Chapter 1, the ERA assigned the Secretary of State the tasks of appointing the membership and establishing the terms of reference for each of the groups that were to advise on the requirements for the different National Curriculum subjects. The Secretary of State had the authority to detail the expected format for working groups' recommendations, the approach that they should take in their work and the timetable within which they were to accomplish this. Furthermore, the government could ultimately accept or reject the advice provided by the groups. The arrangements for curriculum developments at other times and in other countries highlight the absence of neutrality inherent in these arrangements for the development of the National Curriculum for England and Wales. For example, in Australia the federal government invited tenders for the tasks of writing the documents that were to provide the national framework for curriculum development (see Marsh 1994; Penney and Glover 1998). As we will see, the 'terms of reference' for the development of the National Curriculum subjects in England and Wales proved critical in enabling the government to retain control and influence in the development and progressively ensure that its discourses and interests were privileged in the 'official texts'. This situation was by no means unique to physical education. The struggles relating to the content of other National Curriculum subjects have been vividly documented by the then chair of the NCC, Duncan Graham. Graham resigned from this position in the light of the political pressures and constraints faced by the NCC and reflecting on the experience, said 'What I did not appreciate anymore than anyone else at the beginning was that this was a highly political exercise to be played by a new set of rules' (Graham with Tytler 1993: 23).

Both the provision of a specific framework and particular arrangements for development of the National Curriculum can therefore be regarded as important 'frames' for the policy process to follow. They provided a specific discursive agenda for the development of the National Curriculum and structural relationships that openly empowered central government and constrained the ability for other individuals and organisations to challenge that authority. In summary, the conditions in which the NCPE was to be developed were characterised by a dominant restorationist agenda for the curriculum, limited resources for curriculum development, and with central government holding a very clear position of authority in (and apparent control over) the development process. We now turn attention to the ways in which these characteristics and conditions were reflected in the development of the NCPE. In so doing we illustrate many of the theoretical concepts discussed in Chapter 2. In particular we encourage readers to note the significant influence of the arrangements for the development of the NCPE texts, the dynamic relationships evident between policy content and contexts, and the contestation between discourses. In the remainder of this chapter we address the composition of the working group established to advise the government on the content of the NCPE, the terms of reference for their work and the first public report produced by the group outlining their proposals for a NCPE.

Selecting the team

The selection of individuals to write and produce the National Curriculum was critical in determining the particular interests that would subsequently find expression in its texts, or equally fail to do so. In the case of the development of the NCPE, it was also a point at which the relative authority of central government and its political interests in education and physical education became transparent. It was far from insignificant that the ERA granted the Secretary of State the authority to determine the membership of the subject working groups for the development of the National Curriculum and then to specify the terms of reference for their work, but irrespective of this, the selection of the working groups was almost inevitably destined to be a contentious issue in the development of the National Curriculum. As Goodson (1993) has emphasised, subject communities are not homogeneous. Rather, they comprise a collection of different and potentially conflicting interests. Certainly in the United Kingdom, but also elsewhere, physical education is a subject in which this lack of homogeneity has been and remains particularly evident. It is a subject that attempts to embrace a wide range of activities and interests and thus, areas of expertise. 'Sport', 'dance', 'outdoor education' and 'health' have long been identifiable 'lobby groups' within 'the profession' of physical education.

Announcing the membership of the working group for physical education in July 1990 John MacGregor, then the Conservative government's Education Secretary, signalled the *particular* interests that the government had in relation to physical education in schools. Ian Beer, the Headmaster of Harrow, a notable private (fee paying) school, was named as the chair of the group whose task was to advise on a curriculum for implementation in all state (i.e. government-funded) schools. The group then included 'professional sportsmen' (John Fashanu, a professional footballer and Steve Ovett an athlete) and 'representatives from the business world' (from IBM and the National Westminster Bank) alongside 'educationalists'. The educationalists included Elizabeth Murdoch, Head of Chelsea School of Human Movement; Margaret Talbot, Head of Carnegie Physical Education Department at Leeds Polytechnic, a primary school headteacher, two deputy headteachers who were formerly physical education teachers, a professor in geography who had previously contributed to a report on outdoor education, a lecturer who had been a member of a review group on people with disabilities, and the director of an arts education project. Notably absent, therefore, were the individuals who would have been the first people many would turn to for advice on physical education curricula – practising physical education teachers. Thus, specific interests were apparent in the membership, but so were key omissions (see also Evans and Penney 1995b).

The group therefore appeared to be a symbolic representation of what, in the government's view, physical education ought to be. It signalled a blurring of boundaries between physical education and sport, but also their potential dissolution in the interests of the latter. The selection of the chair from a school and education system renowned for its sporting traditions and emphasis on sports performance within the physical education curriculum, indicated the direction of the Conservative government's desires for state education. The appointment of two professional sportsmen reinforced the view that physical education was being equated with sport and that it was seen as virtually exclusively about *performance* in sports. At the same time, the inclusion of representatives from the business world reflected the government's broader agenda for education, of increased 'efficiency' and 'accountability' and for heightened sensitivity to the needs and interests of industry and 'the market' in education.

With its obvious omissions in representation, the composition of the group also indicated the government's view of what physical education should *not* be. While 'sport' was 'empowered', other interests in physical education, for example health education, were essentially excluded. The specific absence of practising physical education teachers had other implicit messages. Exclusion signalled teachers' subordination in the development of the NCPE, but also the conceptualisation of policy 'making' and 'implementation' as distinct activities that should be the responsibility of different groups. Education was clearly something to be delivered but not defined by teachers. Not surprisingly, the logic of some of the selections was questioned by some members of the physical education profession. Commenting on the inclusion of Steve Ovett and John Fashanu in the group, Ken Fox wryly wrote:

I remain puzzled as to whether it is their high degree of sporting talent or their artistry with TV commentary which apparently has given them such valued insight into the needs of children. Their selection seems a bit like asking a Formula 1 racing driver's advice on how to design a new public transport system.

(1992: 8)

The government's team selection thus clearly brought to the surface its agenda for the National Curriculum for Physical Education and revealed that this was a development that was not going to be driven primarily by either the interests of physical educationalists, or any straightforward educational concern. Furthermore, the policy game was one that would definitely be played by the government's rules.

The rules of the game: the terms of reference for the working group

The terms of reference for the NCPE working group confirmed the anticipation that the recommendations for physical education would be less prescriptive than those for other core and foundation subjects within the National Curriculum. The task of the physical education working group was specified as being 'to advise on a statutory framework which is *sufficiently broad and flexible to allow schools wide discretion in relation to the matters to be studied*' (DES 1990: 4, our emphasis). The statutory requirements for PE were to comprise end of key stage statements expressing in 'broad terms' what 'pupils of different abilities and maturities can be expected to achieve at the end of the key stage' (ibid.). In contrast to other curriculum subjects, there would not be statutory statements of attainment for identified levels (1–10). Instead, non-statutory statements of attainment were requested that 'should form part of the guidance to teachers to help them to plan for continuity and progression and to identify both high attainers and those in need of extra help' (ibid.; see also Chapter 1). It thus appeared that the NCPE was to be in Hill's (1980) terms, a 'skeletal policy' that left many decisions relating to what was to comprise the NCPE to those charged with its implementation. Certainly, underpinning the desire for schools to have 'wide discretion' was the need for a structure and requirements with minimal resource implications. In short, the Conservative government needed a National Curriculum that could be implemented within the existing and varied conditions of resourcing in schools. In physical education, these differences are often very significant in terms of the opportunities that may be pursued in curriculum development. Schools are variously advantaged and disadvantaged in the facilities and staff expertise that they can draw upon. As we will see, it was increasingly emphasised that the requirements for the NCPE needed to be able to accommodate such differences.

In both their interim report (DES and Welsh Office (WO) 1991a) and final report (DES and WO 1991b) the NCPE working group highlighted the difficulties that these terms of reference presented for them. They emphasised that 'the remit to provide a less prescriptive structure than for other foundation subjects made our work more rather than less difficult' (DES and WO 1991b: 3). The timescale within which working groups had to operate was another feature of the arrangements for policy development that clearly impacted upon (and restricted) this and other working groups. In the case of physical education, the working group's interim report was required to be submitted to the Secretary of State just five months after their appointment. Six months later their final report was required. The group were advised that they 'should consult informally and selectively with relevant interests' (DES 1990: 5) and that they should also have regard for the developments in other National Curriculum subjects, particularly music and art (ibid.). Who and what were regarded as 'relevant interests' was not defined, but the tight schedule obviously restricted the consultation that was possible and the range of interests that could be considered. One member of the group openly acknowledged that the limited time available restricted the degree to which responses from the group's consultations could be utilised in the development. The 'vast' volume of responses received by the group 'posed a problem of analysis within the time available' (Murdoch 1992: 18).

In important respects, therefore, the conditions for the development of the NCPE seemed restrictive and the group's work looked set to be constrained by the arrangements for policy development established by the ERA. However, in their interim report the group demonstrated that even in apparently 'tight' conditions of policy development, there remained some scope for adaptation, contestation and resistance. There were limits to the 'control' placed upon the group's work. Consequently, as we see, there was capacity for a *variety* of interests to be pursued and for different discourses to emerge, some of which ran counter to the narrow aspirations and expectations of the Conservative government's hopes and thinking for physical education in England and Wales.

Scope for slippage: the interim report

The interim report was the first document to be presented by the group to the Secretary of State and to those who would be faced with implementing the NCPE. As such it was the reference point for the continued development of the NCPE, and was critical in defining the format and content of the NCPE. It was a text that in important respects illustrated the way in which policies create conditions, both boundaries and opportunities, for subsequent policies. It demonstrated how policy texts can set or 'frame' (see Chapter 2) the direction of and for later texts. In the report, and contrary to the expectations of many in the profession and among central government, the working group presented something of a challenge to the government's authority in the policy process. At least to some degree they endorsed a progressive, child-centred view of physical education and openly rejected a narrow, games-focused, restorationist view (see below and also Evans and Penney 1995b). However, in important respects the text of the interim report nevertheless fell very clearly in line with the Conservative government's interests, and it is these latter characteristics that we address first.

Just as the structure of the National Curriculum as a whole (re-) established the traditional and 'obvious' subject-based framework for school curricula, so the interim report for the NCPE identified different *activities* as the central organising theme for physical education. The attainment targets and programmes of study (see Chapter 1) related to six **areas of activity**; games activities, dance forms, gymnastic activities, athletic activities, swimming and water-based activities, and outdoor education and adventure activities (DES and WO 1991a). This structure was presented as a 'natural', non-contestable, *fait accompli*, belying the possibilities that existed for the construction of alternative and/or more integrated curricula. There were alternative frameworks that could have been developed and there is always the potential for curricula to take a different form. We explore these possibilities in more detail in Chapter 7. At this time, however, it seemed that the NCPE working group either had no desire or no apparent opportunity to present a challenge to an activity-based curriculum. Furthermore, it was differences between the various areas of activity, rather than any commonalities between them, that were highlighted in the group's text. The text of the interim report emphasised in Bernstein's terms, a 'collection' rather than 'integrated' code (see also Evans and Penney 1995b). For example, the report stated:

> Dance forms emphasise the artistic and expressive aspects of movement, whereas gymnastic activities demand the control of the body in increasingly challenging situations. Athletic activities pursue individual excellence, where pupils strive to improve performance against measurements and/or others.
>
> (DES and WO 1991a: 61)

The association of a particular emphasis, form of learning and skill with each of these activities is largely arbitrary and can be contested. Each of the activities of the NCPE could claim to facilitate learning across the range of experiences mentioned. However, opportunities for them to do so were, it seems, never explored.

Recognition of the capacity for learning to occur across different areas of activity came in the form of the identification of the 'permeating themes' of (i) health and safety education, (ii) personal and social education, (iii) sensory experience and aesthetic expression and appreciation, and (iv) equal opportunities (DES and WO 1991a). However, these themes were very specifically positioned in the text of the NCPE. Essentially they were framed in a subordinate relation to the areas of activity. With the attainment targets and programmes of study centring on the areas of activity rather than these themes, the interim report signalled that the themes were of secondary concern and status in the development of the NCPE. Reinforcement of this hierarchical structure also arose from *omissions* in the text of the NCPE. The text remained silent on how the themes were to be developed, applied and expressed through the areas of activity. As we will see, from this point on the focus on areas was a seemingly incontestable matter in the development of the NCPE, and to a great extent this was to the exclusion of any consideration of the themes. The interim report had created and legitimated a particular discursive frame for all further development. The debates that followed addressed and contested the requirements and coverage that would exist *within* the area structure, but the structure itself remained essentially unchallenged.

In part the activity-based structure may well have reflected a lack of desire on the part of the working group to 'redefine' the 'established' physical education in the United Kingdom. However, it also signified an acknowledgement on the part of the group of the immense political pressures surrounding the development of the NCPE. As we illustrate in Chapter 4, subsequent actions by the Conservative government indicated that an 'alternative' focus for physical education was not, given the advisory status of the working group, ever going to be a possibility in the development of the NCPE. Quite simply it would not have been acceptable to a government patently driven by a desire to highlight and restore, rather than weaken or erode, traditional boundaries and hierarchies in education (Evans and Penney 1995b). Nor, we suggest, would any 'alternative' have been popular with many physical education teachers. Many teachers have struggled to either accept, or willingly consider, anything other than a curriculum centring on different activities. The historical context of physical education in the United Kingdom and the biographies of teachers conditioned and formed by their own experiences of the collection codes of physical education as pupils, and reinforced in initial teacher training (Evans and Davies 1997), therefore also need to be acknowledged as highly influential in the policy process. Finally, the timescale for the development of the NCPE as defined by the ERA inevitably further constrained and narrowed the agendas and debates, creating a view that there was not the time available to consider a more 'radical' restructuring of the subject. Thus a number of features of the context and arrangements for the development of the NCPE played a part in producing a particular structure for the curriculum outlined in the interim report, and this was then itself a key reference point and frame for the continuing policy process.

So far we have emphasised the conservatism of the interim report; the compatibility of its text with the government's view of 'physical education as sport' and with established practice in the UK. However, we also need to acknowledge important ways in which the production of this text signalled a degree of independence of the working group; their capacity to bring *different* discourses and interests to the foreground, to extend the discursive boundaries of the policy process and arguably to challenge the authority and narrow conservative agendas of central government.

An educational emphasis

The rationale for physical education presented in the interim report stressed the cognitive as well as the practical aspect of the subject and via one of the key structural organisers for all National Curriculum subjects, the attainment targets, the working group made a critical statement about the nature and aims of physical education. The report identified *three* attainment targets as the fundamental components of progressive development in physical education: (i) planning and composing; (ii) participating and performing; and (iii) appreciating and evaluating (DES and WO 1991a). Physical education was thereby clearly identified as about more than *just* performance. Evident here was the influence of an earlier report compiled by the British Council for Physical Education (BCPE) that identified knowing, doing and understanding as the three key components of physical education (BCPE 1990; Evans and Penney 1995a; Penney 1994) but also, the relative influence that different members of the working group had gained within that group. In this and other respects the interim report reflected the dominant role that the *educationalists* in the group had assumed. It was they, rather than the appointed representatives of sport, for example, who seemed to now have a degree of authority and control of the development (Evans and Penney 1995b).

It was equally notable that the rationale for physical education identified the curriculum as centring on the child and children's physical, mental, social and emotional development, as distinct from a view of physical education as essentially about performance in specific activities (sports and particularly team games) achieved through the attainment of specific skills. As we have indicated above, the irony and apparent contradiction was that the report then provided an activity-based structure for the curriculum. This, together with the working group's identification of the second attainment target, 'Participating and Performing', as 'the single most important element of attainment within physical education'

(DES and WO 1991a: 26), served to indicate that there were limits to the 'resistance' that could be displayed. As we will see, pressures and constraints upon the group's work became increasingly explicit.

The other key respect in which the interim report could be regarded as having a distinct educational commitment and orientation was in the range of different activities that it emphasised that children should experience in physical education. It was recommended that pupils should experience all six areas of activity in key stages 1 (from age 4 to 7), 2 (from age 7 to 11) and 3 (from age 11 to 14), and at least three areas including games and either gymnastics or dance in key stage 4 (from age 14 to 16). These requirements were openly directed towards encouraging greater balance between different activities in physical education curricula and a move away from the long established bias in many schools, of games dominating the physical education curriculum. The working group also made it clear that educational interests of children should be considered over and above pragmatic and economic concerns in the development of the NCPE. Ian Beer indicated the group's awareness of the government's concerns about the resource implications of recommendations, but also their resistance to the narrow direction in which the curriculum could be driven if directed by these concerns. Commenting on the group's proposals for the inclusion of swimming and outdoor education in the NCPE he stated:

> We do of course appreciate the resource implications of these recommendations. However, after very careful consideration we concluded that these two elements of physical education were too important to leave to chance and should be an entitlement for all young people under the National Curriculum.
>
> (Beer 1991)

Although this statement can be seen as signalling the group's resistance to the government's discourse of pragmatism, paradoxically, in making *any* reference to these concerns, the group unintentionally gave pragmatism legitimacy. As we will see, this discourse was secured a place and gained an increasingly high profile in the debates that followed the publication of the interim report.

While drawing attention to the group's emphasis on range and breadth in the curriculum, it is also appropriate here to note some of the arrangements for the development of the NCPE. The working group had neither the authority nor scope to define the time to be allocated to either physical education as a whole, or any of its constituent parts. These were matters upon which individual schools would make decisions. The balance between the different areas of activity and what constituted the NCPE in different schools, could clearly vary greatly. Certainly, there would be scope for slippage during the implementation of the NCPE.

Conclusion

The interim report from the working group appointed to advise the Conservative government on the NCPE was thus a significant, contested and contestable policy text. It expressed and reflected a complex mix of interests and associated discourses at play in the policy process; the educational, the established and restorationist interests in physical education and pragmatic concerns. The report legitimated key discourses, particularly in its privileging of the areas of activity and its acknowledgement that resource implications were to be considered alongside educational concerns. At the same time, however, it was a text that signalled the group's resistance and freedom from constraint in the policy process. The child-centred rationale, the identification of three attainment targets and the emphasis of the need for breadth of experience in physical education gave the text a notably progressive feel. In the following chapter we see ways in which this emphasis was to a large extent lost and subordinated as the development of the NCPE progressed and as the interim report was superseded by new texts.

Summary

The National Curriculum was a key aspect of the Conservative government's response to the claimed 'crisis' in education. Notably, rather than proposing a new direction and structure for school curricula, the National Curriculum provided a framework for (re-)establishing familiar and traditional subject based curricula. Physical education was arguably accorded a low status as a foundation subject placed late in the phased development process. At the same time, however, it was a subject of clear political interest. This was reflected first in the selection of the working group appointed to advise the government on the content of the National Curriculum for Physical Education. Interests of 'sport' seemed particularly privileged, while physical education teachers were a notable omission among the membership. The first report produced by the working group contained elements of conservatism (in particular presenting a structure for the curriculum centring upon familiar areas of activity) but also clearly privileged educational interests (emphasising a central focus on the child; identifying planning, performing and evaluating as three core and interrelated dimensions of physical education, and encouraging a range of experiences in the curriculum). The report emphasised that educational concerns, over and above pragmatic issues, should frame the NCPE. As such, it was a text that challenged the Conservative government's agenda for policy and practice in physical education in England and Wales.

Further reading

For further commentary on the development of the National Curriculum as a whole, see for example:

Kelly, A.V. (1990) *The National Curriculum. A Critical Review*. London: Paul Chapman Publishing Ltd.
Graham, D. with Tytler, D. (1993) *A Lesson for Us All. The Making of the National Curriculum*. London: Routledge.

Previous works by ourselves provides additional details of the actions of the working group for physical education and our theorisation of this. See in particular:

Evans, J. and Penney, D. (1995) 'The Politics of Pedagogy: Making a National Curriculum Physical Education', *Journal of Education Policy* 10(1): 27–44.
Evans, J. and Penney, D. (1995) 'Physical Education, Restoration and the Politics of Sport', *Curriculum Studies*, 3(2): 183–196.

In addition, some members of the NCPE working group have provided commentary on the development. See for example:

Murdoch, E.B. (1992) 'Physical Education Today', *The Bulletin of Physical Education*, 28(2): 15–24.
Talbot, M. (1993) 'Physical Education and the National Curriculum: Some Political Issues' in G. McFee and A. Tomlinson (eds) *Education, Sport and Leisure: Connections and Controversies*. Eastbourne: Chelsea School Research Centre, University of Brighton.

Chapter 4

Stopping the slippage and redirecting the play

In the previous chapter we indicated the significance of the interim report in establishing a particular structure (and discursive frames, see Chapter 2) for the NCPE. However, the response to that report from the Secretary of State for Education had even greater implications for the subsequent development of the NCPE. This response indicated quite clearly that the government was far from satisfied with the recommendations in the interim report. Furthermore, it detailed the modifications to the structure and content of the curriculum that, in the government's view, were now required. The response made very clear the inequalities inherent in the policy process in terms of the relative authority of different players in that process, and drew attention to the significance of the arrangements for policy that the government had established in the ERA. In essence the nature and tone of the Secretary of State's comments signalled the authoritative and uncompromising position of central government and indicated that its interests were, to a great extent, not open to negotiation.

The Secretary of State's response to the working group's interim report also needs to be seen as the starting point of a process in which the NCPE underwent a transformation, from a text clearly containing elements of progressivism and concern for educational issues, to one in which these discourses were subordinated and displaced by those of pragmatism and cultural restoration. Progressively, a very different view and definition of physical education to that expressed in the interim report was established as the basis for the NCPE, with attention centring on performance, especially in 'traditional' team games. Below we describe in detail the various phases of this transformation, drawing attention to the significance of the arrangements for policy development, the critical interaction between texts and contexts, and the influence of 'discourses surrounding discourses' (see Chapter 2) in the policy development. As we will see, as well as signalling the increasingly limited authority of the working group, the events following the publication of the interim report also highlighted the marginal position of teachers in the policy process. We cover a lot of ground in this chapter as we attempt to highlight the links between the different stages of the development of the NCPE and explore both the continuities and contrasts between the various texts produced.

'Practical' concerns

There were two key features to the government's response to the interim report that ironically, were the basis of a paradox that remained throughout the development of the NCPE. On the one hand there was pressure for increased *prescription* in relation to the inclusion of games in the physical education curriculum. On the other, the government emphasised the need for *flexibility* in requirements to accommodate the different school contexts (in terms of facilities and staff expertise, particularly) in which implementation would occur, and to minimise the resource implications of meeting requirements. With respect to this latter concern, Kenneth Clarke, the then Secretary of State for Education, 'reminded' the working group that the programmes of study for physical education should 'not be too detailed and should contribute to a sensible non-prescriptive statutory framework for PE' (Clarke 1991). He specifically questioned the recommended inclusion of all six areas of activity in key stage 3, suggesting that, instead, schools may choose four out of the six areas at this stage. In addition he identified the requirements for key stage 4 as needing greater flexibility. He explained 'I have it in mind that pupils should have the choice of two or even one of the areas of activity', and went on to stress the 'serious practical implications for many schools' of the group's proposals for swimming, dance and outdoor education. Casting doubt on the inclusion of these areas in the NCPE, he stated that he would 'need to consider them in the light of what you and those commenting on your report have to say about their feasibility' (ibid.). For 'practical reasons' he also rejected the recommendation that a residential experience should be an obligatory part of the PE curriculum and asked the group 'to reconsider the feasibility of compulsory inclusion of outdoor education in the statutory PE curriculum' (ibid., 1991). In case he had left the working group in any doubts as to what was now required of them, Clarke emphasised that:

> It is not part of the Group's remit to make recommendations for the resources to be provided for PE. I expect your recommendations to be realistically related to the general level of school funding which can reasonably be expected to be available.
>
> (Ibid.)

In addition he reiterated the government's refusal to make any recommendation with respect to the curriculum *time* allocated to physical education. He stressed that this was a matter for schools to decide and that he therefore saw:

... no need for you to pursue the matter of time allocation, except in the sense that you should have regard to what is likely to be practicable within the constraints of school timetables and the rest of the curriculum.

(Ibid.)

As well as these pragmatic and economically driven concerns, the government's ideological interests relating to physical education were explicit in the Secretary of State's response to the working group. He openly challenged the rationale privileged in the interim report, saying that he was 'not at all convinced' by the structure for physical education provided by the three attainment targets and requested that the group reconsider this 'with a view to coming up with a *single attainment target* for physical education which reflects the *practical nature of the subject*' (Clarke 1991, our emphasis). He added 'I should be grateful if you could ensure that the *active element* is predominant' (ibid., our emphasis). Similarly he reminded the working group that the programmes of study 'should focus on the active side of PE' (ibid.). He also criticised the language used in the report, saying that the working group had failed to avoid using 'jargon'. He stressed the need for the text (and particularly the titles of the attainment targets) to 'be readily understood by non-specialist teachers, parents and pupils' (ibid.). These comments, which struck at the heart of the professional identity of physical education, reflected the difference between the Secretary of State's conception of physical education and that articulated in the interim report. The Secretary of State's 'back to basics' view of physical education privileged team games and sport performance, while the working group had at least to some extent privileged a child-centred educational rationale and the notion of 'breadth and balance' in the curriculum. The interim report had presented an altogether more liberal and comprehensive view of physical education than the government could either relate to, or would accept, for the NCPE.

The spectators' views

The Secretary of State was not the only person to have something to say about the interim report. Its publication was also an important first opportunity for others (particularly physical education professional associations and teachers) to voice their views and opinions about the structure and content of the NCPE. However, our research highlighted that there were limits to this opportunity and clear constraints in the consultation processes. Under the terms of the ERA, the Secretary of State could withhold the publication of working group reports, reject their proposals or even disband a group if he wished. The interim report for the NCPE was expected in January 1991 but its release was delayed until February.

Clearly a delay at any stage of an already rushed development restricted opportunities for consultation and debate. In addition, consultation and debate was set within a quite specific framework. It was open to only a limited audience and was 'guided' by a centrally imposed restricted agenda. The interim report was sent to all Local Education Authorities (LEAs) and 'a wide range of organisations with an inherent interest in physical education' (DES and WO 1991b: 10). Physical education teachers, however, had to request a copy if they wanted to see the proposals and make a response, if indeed they were even aware of the existence of the report. The format, desired content and time limit for responses were all arguably restrictive aspects of the consultation. Notably there was apparently not the scope to question the overlying structure of the NCPE. The focus was on modifications to the requirements within the established structure, rather than consideration of any alternatives to it. There seemed to be no possibility for consultees to extend the discursive frames that had been established in the policy process. It is also significant that LEAs were assigned responsibility for co-ordinating teachers' responses to the report. In the following chapter we examine one LEA's response to the interim report and in so doing, illustrate the impact of this indirect line of communication in the policy process. We highlight that the arrangements for consultation in effect positioned people very differently in the policy game.

The responses received by the Department for Education and Science (DES) highlighted a clear lack of consensus about the appropriate structure, content and language for the NCPE. To some extent differences in opinions on these issues were associated with fundamental differences in the conceptualisation of physical education. Organisations and individuals from 'sport' echoed the Secretary of State's criticism of the language of the report (British Institute of Sports Coaches (BISC) 1991; McNab 1992; National Coaching Foundation (NCF) 1991) and his call for a greater practical emphasis in the text (BISC 1991; McNab 1992; see Penney 1994). Tom McNab, then the vice-chair of the British Institute of Sports Coaches (BISC), described the interim report as a 'jargon-ridden, defensive document' and called for the development of a 'realistic, practical and predominantly physical curriculum' (McNab 1992: 4). The Central Council of Physical Recreation (CCPR) expressed concern with respect to the time that would be devoted to sport in the curriculum and therefore the future of 'our major team games' (CCPR 1991). BISC (1991) supported the Secretary of State's request for a single attainment target.

Representatives of the 'health lobby' attacked the report from a different perspective and were critical of the 'permeation model' proposed as the basis for addressing health in the NCPE. This approach was described as one which 'marginalises Health Related Exercise and causes it to take second place to other issues' (Health Education Authority (HEA)/Physical

Education Association (PEA) 1991: 2). Health related exercise (HRE) concepts were highlighted as being too important 'to be left "floating" amongst a very conventional range of activity areas' (ibid.). The concerns about this status and 'location' for health anticipated the potential 'loss' of this and other themes in implementation. These fears seem to have been well justified. Edwards (1995) has identified that the strength of classification (Bernstein 1971, 1990) and boundaries between subjects in the National Curriculum as a whole has meant that cross-curricular themes have 'struggled to survive' or have been 'so permeated' that most pupils are 'unaware of having learned anything about them at all' (Edwards 1995: 109). Apparently anxious for a more secure place for health in physical education, some teachers questioned where successful developments of HRE units of work could be placed in the NCPE (Penney 1994). By contrast, however, some within the 'dance lobby' continued to question the appropriateness and merits of the identification of dance as an area of activity within physical education, and sought a break from the subject, rather than a stronger position within it (Talbot 1993).

In contrast to these criticisms, responses from 'physical education' professional groups stressed support for the working group and in particular for the rationale presented in the interim report (British Association of Advisers and Lecturers in Physical Education (BAALPE) 1991a; BCPE 1991; HEA/PEA 1991; PEA 1991). Most of these organisations also expressed strong support for a structure based on the three attainment targets (BAALPE 1991a; BCPE 1991; HEA/PEA 1991; Standing Conference on Physical Education in Teacher Education (SCOPE) 1991a). An underlying concern for these organisations was that a reduction to a single attainment target may lead not only to the 'loss' of the elements addressing planning and evaluation, but also to corresponding reductions in curriculum time for physical education. Educational and pragmatic concerns thus coincided. At the same time, however, members of physical education associations acknowledged that it was impossible to separate the three specified components of physical education and stressed that planning and composing, and evaluation and assessment should 'permeate' performance (Penney 1994). In the PEA's view, the *number* of attainment targets was not the issue, it was rather that 'the active nature and the process of learning associated with the subject' should be reflected (PEA 1991: 1).

While stressing support for the proposals, representatives of physical education also expressed some concerns about the prospects of implementation. In so doing they highlighted a dilemma of wanting to establish 'the ideal' in policy while at the same time recognising the need for the requirements to also reflect 'realism', i.e. the limits of current practice and resourcing in schools. In essence a pragmatic discourse had to accompany and be embedded in an educational one. The PEA (1991) drew attention to concerns about the manageability of the proposals for primary schools particularly, and suggested 'clustering' the areas of activity in key stages 1 and 2. The structure of the programmes of study at key stages 1 and 2 was regarded as problematic for both delivery in schools and initial teacher training. Staff from teacher training institutions indicated that they could provide *experience* in all areas, but that the time available for physical education within training courses was insufficient for student teachers to achieve *competence or expertise* in all areas. The requirements for key stage 3, and specifically the inclusion of dance and outdoor education were also identified as demanding changes in secondary initial teacher training (Penney 1994).

Physical education teachers[1] similarly faced a dilemma in responding to the interim report, of on the one hand wanting to voice support for what they regarded as a good outline of 'the ideal' curriculum for physical education, but at the same time being aware that 'in reality' they would not have the resources of curriculum time, staff expertise, facilities or finance to deliver this, particularly in primary schools. Primary teachers drew attention to the problems that they could foresee in the requirement to cover all six areas, and staffing of outdoor education and dance were regarded as particularly problematic for both primary and secondary schools. These were the two areas of activity in which teachers felt in-service training would be essential. An appreciation of the desirability of these activities was accompanied by concerns that neither the time nor the funding required for training would be forthcoming. The tension between educational and pragmatic concerns was thus very evident in teachers' responses, as was the way in which contexts of implementation were framing opinions about policy content. This was similarly the case in relation to the recommendations for swimming. Teachers drew attention to the fact that in many schools the time taken to travel to a swimming pool meant that the length of timetable periods was unsuitable for the inclusion of swimming in the physical education curriculum. In addition, the requirement to include swimming was acknowledged as having significant financial implications for schools. However, these concerns were mediated and tempered by educational interests. The BCPE expressed the view that the proposals should not be sacrificed because of these implications, saying that:

> Swimming may demand extra resourcing but, as a genuine life-skill, some access to learning needs to be offered and water safety principles taught to all. Questioning the proposals of the subject working

---

1 As explained in Chapter 1, at this time our research focused on teachers within one Local Education Authority in England. Their response to the interim report is addressed in more detail in Chapter 5.

group challenges the concept of entitlement, a principle on which the 1988 Act is based.

(1991: 3)

Others, however, gave more weight to pragmatic concerns. For example, the then executive secretary of the National Coaching Foundation stated 'I fully support the inclusion of swimming and outdoor education in the curriculum but question whether or not this can be financed in the present climate' (NCF 1991).

Looking ahead to implementation, teachers also called for the text of the NCPE to include more and better examples of what they were required to do, and how. For example, they wanted specific and explicit guidance on how assessment was to be conducted and what aspects of learning in physical education were to be reported on (Penney 1994). Guidance on these and other matters, such as how permeating themes were to be developed in curricula, were notable omissions in the text of the interim report. However, there were also omissions in the responses to the report. Although we saw some differences in the various responses and deviations from the agenda set by the Secretary of State's response, overall the responses were strongly framed by the Secretary of State's letter. His response had ensured that much of the content of the report was ignored or overlooked in debates following its publication and that in the main, issues of resourcing physical education were foregrounded and educational issues subordinated. With the exception of health, the 'permeating themes' appeared to be either forgotten or ignored. Discussion of the programmes of study centred on matters of the practicality of including the various areas of activity in the curriculum, rather than the educational rationale for their inclusion or the pedagogies that could or should be pursued in their development. The differences of opinion expressed about these matters signalled the prospect of continued contestation in the development of the NCPE, but the agenda for its further development had been firmly set. Furthermore, in privileging these discourses, the responses to the interim report served to legitimate the government's discourses in the development of the NCPE, and signalled acceptance of rather than resistance to this discursive frame.

There was also an important degree to which the working group's adoption of the government's interests was 'non-negotiable'. This was reflected in the amendments that the group made to their recommendations following these reactions to the interim report. The arrangements for policy were such that strategically, the group's best approach was not only to adopt, but to explicitly privilege the government's interests and discourses and within these, attempt to retain some elements of the progressivism and educational focus that the interim report had expressed. They had little choice. Failure to take such an approach was likely to result in the group being replaced by writers who would take the stance desired by the government and who may not share the same concern for educational issues (Evans and Penney 1995b; Graham with Tytler 1993; Talbot 1993).

The final report for the NCPE: compromise and control in the policy process

The working group's final report published on 21 August 1991 therefore featured significant changes to the format and content of the NCPE presented in the interim report. The working group chair's introductory letter to the Secretary of State stressed that notable modifications had been made to their earlier proposals in the light of the concerns expressed by the Secretary of State. The significance of these modifications for the NCPE should not be under-estimated. The final report formally redirected the development of the NCPE, and redefined physical education in this process.

After much deliberation the working group had concluded that the three elements identified as attainment targets in the interim report could be encompassed in a single attainment target. The interrelated nature of the three elements became the focus of the rationale presented for a structure with a single attainment target. In accordance with the Secretary of State's demands, it was stressed that 'The emphasis should always be on active participation' with the other two elements being pursued through this (DES and WO 1991b: 17). The group left the single attainment target nameless, instead defining it as comprising the end of key stage statements for each of the four key stages. As had been requested in the terms of reference (see Chapter 1), these statements were 'general' in nature. For example, the end of key stage statements for key stage 3 stated that pupils should be able to show that they can:

- devise and improvise strategies and tactics across appropriate activities within the programmes of study;
- adapt and refine existing skills and develop new skills across the activities in the programmes of study;
- rehearse and present movement compositions devised by themselves and others across appropriate activities in the programmes of study;
- evaluate how well they and others have achieved what they set out to do, appreciate strengths and weaknesses and suggest ways of improving; and
- understand the short and long term effects of exercise on the body and decide where to focus their involvement in physical activity for a healthy and enjoyable lifestyle.

(DES and WO 1991b: 19)

The only clearly prescriptive end of key stage statement related to swimming. It was stated that pupils should be able to 'swim at least 25 metres and demonstrate an understanding of water safety' by the end of key stage 2 (ibid.).

The final report also made marked changes to the requirements relating to the programmes of study. The increased flexibility of the recommendations was stressed. Although the structure of six areas of activity was maintained for key stages 1 and 2, schools were now to be free to choose whether they taught swimming during key stage 1, during key stage 2, or across both key stages (DES and WO 1991b). Meanwhile for key stages 3 and 4, the six areas of activity were re-grouped into five areas, with swimming and water-based activities essentially relocated within the other areas. The working group explained that competitive swimming, for example, could occur within athletic activities, or water polo within games. Their recommendation for key stage 3 was that all five areas of activity should be experienced during the key stage, but that at least four areas should be addressed in any one school year, one of which must be dance or gymnastic activities, and one games. At key stage 4 it was recommended that pupils not taking a GCSE[2] in physical education or a related area should study at least two activities. These could be drawn from the same area of activity, 'for example, two games such as hockey and cricket or two gymnastic activities such as rhythmic gymnastics and trampolining', or from two different areas (ibid.: 25–26).

Responding to the concerns for both minimal resource implications and a 'physical' focus in the NCPE, the working group also renamed the area 'outdoor education and adventure activities' 'outdoor and adventurous activities'. The group explained that they regarded outdoor education as an issue that needed to be addressed in relation to the curriculum as a whole, not only in physical education, and that therefore they had:

> ... decided to limit the scope of our recommendations to those aspects of outdoor education which are clearly part of physical education. By this we mean the 'outdoor and adventurous activities' that are almost entirely physical in content, such as orienteering, rock climbing, skiing ...
>
> (DES and WO 1991b: 12)

The report also explained that because of the practical implications arising, they had removed the recommendation that a residential experience be a statutory requirement within the National Curriculum.

---

2 General Certificate in Secondary Education, i.e. an optional examination subject.

The commitment to breadth and balance of experiences in physical education that had been stressed in the interim report was clearly compromised by these amendments and it was evident that, increasingly, pragmatic rather than educational issues were the primary concern in the development of the NCPE. In addition, however, these revisions to the requirements privileged certain areas of activity over and above others and signalled the *unequal status* in the policy process of the various interests within physical education.

The legitimation and privileging of pragmatic concerns over and above educational matters was also evident elsewhere in the report. Balance was clearly identified as a *secondary* consideration in curriculum design, with the working group explaining that the choice of activities offered 'should depend *largely* on what schools are able to offer, but should *also* have regard to the principle of balance' (ibid.: 26, our emphasis). Similarly, the report stressed that the different areas need not receive equal attention. It explained that allocations to different areas would reflect that 'Children's physical development demands different emphases on different activities at different times', but also *'practical considerations*, such as travelling time' (ibid.: 27, our emphasis).

The working group devoted a chapter of the report to specifically addressing the issues highlighted by the Secretary of State in his response to their interim report, and another to the 'general resource implications' of the recommendations in the final report. In the former they stressed the extent to which they had pursued the government's concerns about resourcing and modified their proposals accordingly. They stressed that existing levels of resourcing would enable *most* schools to meet the demands of the proposals, particularly in the secondary sector. Facility and grounds maintenance, and non-specialist staffing of physical education were identified as problems likely to arise in *some* schools, but the emphasis was on the 'general adequacy' of existing physical and human resources in secondary schools, and the *limited* investment that was therefore required for implementation. Similarly, the resource implications of the recommendations relating to dance and swimming were identified as being minimal and relatively easily addressed. With respect to dance, the report stated that '66 per cent of the primary schools surveyed and 45 per cent of secondary believed that they already had adequate physical resources to provide dance in key stages 1–3' (DES and WO 1991b: 11). The text did not address the situation of the 55 per cent of secondary schools not making this response. Likewise, it was stated that only a minority of schools faced problems with respect to access to a swimming pool. It was acknowledged that the proposals for swimming would give rise to 'some additional costs' but in the working group's view these did not need to be prohibitive; 'with good planning and effective timetabling, it is perfectly practicable for swimming to be a compulsory part of the curriculum' (ibid.: 51).

At the same time, however, there was clear recognition that primary schools lacked both the physical and human resources needed to 'deliver' the group's recommendations for key stages 1 and 2. The report stated:

> There is no doubt that some primary schools will find it difficult to implement all aspects of the programmes of study. . . . 10 per cent of primary schools are without fixed gymnastic apparatus, and in some cases where the apparatus does exist it is not always appropriate to the age range.
>
> (Ibid.)

Shortcomings in the physical education expertise of primary teachers, and the support available to them, were also stressed and it was specifically noted that 'in-service training in dance and outdoor and adventurous activities will be particularly important for primary teachers' (ibid.; see also Chapter 5).

Overall, the final report seemed a substantial 'surrender' to the Secretary of State's demands. It could not have been otherwise. The power relations at work in the policy process had strongly framed the working group's ability to resist, adapt or reject the interests expressed by the Secretary of State. The modifications they made to the NCPE text had inherent 'costs'. The final report further narrowed the agenda for the continued development of the NCPE and signalled the subordination of educational discourses. Characteristics that had identified the interim report as progressive in educational terms (particularly the emphasis of planning and evaluating alongside performing) were now implicit rather than explicit in the text. Now marginalised, the degree to which these interests would find expression in the practice developed by schools was questionable. In adopting the government's agenda the final report also presaged an increased emphasis upon the performance aspects of physical education, and an acceptance of resourcing as a central issue in curriculum design. Yet despite these changes to the NCPE text, in the government's view the working group had still not adequately addressed the points raised in the Secretary of State's response to the interim report. Consequently, following the publication of the final report and with the working group disbanded (see next section), further changes were made that reaffirmed both the strength of the government's interest in the subject and the control and authority that it could exercise via the arrangements for the development of the National Curriculum.

A change in the players

The further development of the NCPE was now out of the hands of the working group. According to the 'rules of the game', the National

Curriculum Council (NCC) and its parallel organisation in Wales, the Curriculum Council for Wales (CCW) would conduct a consultation on the final report and then report to the Secretary of State. Ministers would then produce 'draft orders' for the National Curriculum for Physical Education, and after a final consultation period, these would be finalised by the Secretary of State and put to parliament. At this stage of the development of the NCPE the prospect of further political pressure and 'direction' in the policy process became immediately apparent. The Secretary of State indicated his continued dissatisfaction with the working group's recommendations in the 'suggestions' that he made to the NCC and CCW for their work. The NCC and CCW were 'invited' to 'consider whether and if so how' the programmes of study 'might be made less detailed' and whether those for key stage 3 were 'too prescriptive in that they require all five areas of activity to be compulsory' (DES and WO 1991b: iv). Additionally it was stated that they would 'want to consider further' whether the requirements relating to swimming could be introduced at the same time as the rest of the NCPE. This latter comment seemed to acknowledge that the NCC and CCW may well offer strong support for the inclusion of swimming, confounding the government's concerns about its resourcing. Delaying the introduction of swimming seemed an obvious 'get out' for the government while avoiding open confrontation with all involved.

Just as the scope for the working group to now play an active role in the 'resolution' of the remaining conflicts and contestation had diminished, so had the potential for other individuals and organisations to influence the further development of the NCPE. Although responses to the NCPE text were again invited, once more there were subtle constraints at play in the policy process and deliberations were constrained by central government's discursive frames. Responses were required within two months, a tight timeframe given that the request came at the start of the academic year when teachers faced the demands of new intakes and timetables. In addition, respondents were required to address a limited number of specific points, concerned with four aspects of the proposals: the attainment target; end of key stage statements; programmes of study; and non-statutory matters (see Penney 1994).

The working group's proposal for a single attainment target in physical education received considerable support (NCC 1991). One of the physical education professional associations expressed its concern that the balance between the three elements needed to be emphasised in the text (BAALPE 1991b), clearly anticipating that the reduction to a single attainment target would result in the 'loss' of planning and evaluating. With respect to the proposed programmes of study, the responses from the professional associations indicated their clear concerns in relation to the matters of breadth and balance within physical education. BAALPE supported the inclusion of six areas at key stages 1 and 2, stressed the need for a range of activities at key stage 3 and therefore also supported the proposal for five areas of activity to be compulsory (BAALPE 1991b). SCOPE (1991b) called for a reversion to six areas at key stage 3 (with swimming identified as a distinct area rather than incorporated within others) stating that this would increase the flexibility at this key stage. Both organisations considered the proposals for key stage 4 as *unlikely to ensure balance* in the physical education curriculum at this key stage. SCOPE (1991b) specifically called for the requirement at key stage 4 to be for pupils to experience two activities from *different* areas. The proposals for swimming were supported (BAALPE 1991b; LEA 1991a;[3] SCOPE 1991b) and the PE organisations *saw no reason* for delaying implementation of this aspect of the NCPE (BAALPE 1991b; SCOPE 1991b; see also Penney 1994).

The health 'lobby' again voiced serious concerns about the overlaying structure of the curriculum. In the view of one representative the proposals offered 'a set of well thought out objectives and outcomes, but an inadequate structure for their delivery' (Fox 1992: 10). Fox explained:

Although health-related concepts should always be reinforced through other activities, they will always remain incidental and superficial unless at some point they provide the central focus in a distinct programme of study.

(Ibid.)

The physical education professional associations also repeated their concerns that, alone, the end of key stage statements did not provide an adequate basis either for assessment or for ensuring progression in the curriculum (BAALPE 1991b; SCOPE 1991b). In their view, statements of attainment (see Chapter 1) were vital in establishing a link between the end of key stage statements and the programmes of study, and should therefore also be statutory (Penney 1994).

Speaking 'on behalf' of teachers in its authority, the response from one LEA (see Chapter 5) reflected teachers' increasing focus on the *pragmatics* of forthcoming implementation. The LEA (1991a) explained that:

. . . teachers are very supportive of the final report for physical education. There is concern, however, that there are implications for funding,

---

3 To retain the anonymity of the authorities who have enabled us access, the referencing of documents issued by them has necessarily been amended. The LEA documents referenced are listed in Appendix B rather than the main bibliography.

resourcing and in particular in-service training and initial teacher training, if the proposals are to be fully implemented.

(cited in Penney 1994: 150)

It stressed that 'Appropriate support within non-statutory guidance, together with INSET opportunities and sufficient resources, must be made available' (LEA 1991a, ibid.). This was a notable shift in the discourses privileged by the LEA, with teachers' pragmatic concerns now openly acknowledged in the LEA text. At this late stage of development of the NCPE, LEAs were more conscious of the need to address problems that could arise in the implementation that they would be overseeing and for which they would be held responsible (see Chapter 5). Clearly, in their view it was now time to put aside more ambitious educational ideals in order to address the harsher realities of implementing the NCPE in schools.

The NCC consultation report and draft orders for the NCPE

The consultation report produced by the NCC showed once again the gross inequalities in the relative capacity for different individuals and organisations to influence policy development. Needless to say, the overriding 'authority' of the Conservative government's interests was very apparent. The statement from the chair of the NCC, David Pascall, that 'In broad terms Council endorses the proposals and has made few key changes to an excellent report' (Pascall 1991) obscured the fact that the text of the consultation report was significantly different to that of the final report. Even greater emphasis was now given to the matter of resourcing physical education and the performance emphasis of the subject, and changes to the working group's recommendations were justified on these grounds.

The recommended programmes of study for key stage 1 and 2 were endorsed by the NCC, but because of the need for further evidence of the resource implications, it stated that a commencement date for swimming in the NCPE could not be recommended. The report stated that swimming should be introduced 'as soon as practicable in order to raise swimming standards in primary schools' (NCC 1991: 7).

The recommendations for key stage 3 were deemed to be 'too prescriptive' (NCC 1991). It was stated that:

In the interest of greater flexibility, Council recommends that pupils should experience a minimum of *four of the five activities by the end of Key Stage 3, games being the only compulsory activity in each year.*

(Ibid.: 14, our emphasis)

This recommendation clearly raised the profile and status of games and appeared to conflict with the statement that:

> Council believes that the provision it is recommending for Key stage 3 retains the principle of breadth and balance in the physical education curriculum provided that each of four activities is covered for a reasonable time by the end of the key stage.
>
> (Ibid.)

While the NCC (1991) described their modifications to the programmes of study as 'not substantial', the likelihood that the NCPE would ensure that all children received a broad and balanced curriculum of physical education had been notably diminished (Talbot 1992). Calls for the activities experienced in key stage 4 to be from *different* areas were ignored. The NCC endorsed the recommendation in the final report that pupils not taking GCSE PE should experience two activities from the same or different areas of activity in key stage 4. The text of the NCC report also made explicit the ideological interests driving these modifications to the NCPE text, and specifically the Conservative government's cultural restorationist interests. The requirement for games to be included in each year of key stage 3 was described as having 'the advantage of perpetuating the best of English [sic] traditions and cultural heritage' (NCC 1991: 14), apparently overlooking the diversity of physical cultures in England, and completely ignoring the Welsh interests and traditions.

The NCPE now seemed 'minimalist' in form, content and quality. As one of the members of the working group later reflected 'in the simplification process much of what was good in the early documents has been lost' (Murdoch 1992: 15). Also now absent from the text of the NCPE was the explicit attention given in earlier texts to a rationale for physical education and matters such as equal opportunities. Murdoch's advice to those facing implementation was 'to consider the documents as *a set* and to make reference as appropriate to the details required' (ibid.). However, not all teachers had seen or in future would be able to access the earlier texts and thus draw on the material they contained. Copies of the working group's reports were increasingly hard to acquire and much of our research has pointed to their content being 'lost' as these texts were superseded in the policy process.

Following the publication of the NCC report, the scope for contesting or changing the proposals for the NCPE was severely restricted. The Secretary of State produced draft orders that were virtually a replication of the NCC report. Copies of the draft orders were sent to the NCC and to all the organisations it had consulted (including Local Education Authorities, organisations representing teachers, headteachers, parents and industry, and professional associations), and one month was allowed for further comments before laying the orders before parliament. Essentially all the NCPE was now lacking was parliament's 'rubber stamp' for the proposals. With a general election pending, the NCPE was quietly 'rushed through' parliament and the statutory orders were published in April 1992 (DES and WO 1992). Implementation of the requirements for key stages 1, 2 and 3 was due to commence in September 1992 (with the exception of those for swimming) and for key stage 4 in 1995. The implementation of the programmes of study for swimming was delayed until 1994. In Chapter 6 we highlight the implications of this tight timescale for the further development of the NCPE. Here we reflect on the 'skeletal' (Hill 1980) nature of the orders.

The inherent flexibility of the requirements seemed to present the scope for considerable variation in the curriculum that would be 'delivered' in schools. The text appeared to present those groups (and particularly teachers) whose influence had been limited during the 'production' of the NCPE texts, with an opportunity now to contest and adapt its content if they so wished. One of the working group expressed the view that 'flexibility can be seen as a strength in that it allows us to make our own interpretations of the document' (Murdoch 1992: 16), but at the same time acknowledged that there was the 'danger of giving mixed messages to teachers and thus losing the potential impact of a coherent and shared curriculum' (ibid.). The degree to which the National Curriculum would produce standardisation in the curricula, teaching and learning of physical education was clearly limited. The exception was its element of prescription relating to the inclusion of games in physical education. However, as well as presenting the potential for creativity, adaptation and resistance among those charged with implementation, the flexibility also allowed for the further influence of economic and pragmatic concerns. Furthermore, it meant that, to a large extent, the demands for *changes* to curricula and teaching practices were minimal. The structure and the inherent bias of the NCPE mirrored that already established in physical education in England and Wales. As we will see, in these conditions the slippage inherent in implementation could have very different connotations to the *deviation* from policy texts with which it has often been associated (see Bowe *et al.* 1992).

At this point we also need to note the promise from the NCC that non-statutory guidance (NSG) would follow the distribution of the orders. There was clearly a danger that in following rather than accompanying the statutory orders, the NSG and therefore the matters that it addressed (such as cross-curricular issues and special educational needs), would be largely overlooked. Implementation was urgent and would already be under way (Penney 1994), and being non-statutory, such guidance would always be liable to be ignored. We need to acknowledge that 'the general perception in schools is that the National Curriculum guidance is of much lesser significance than the subject Orders' (Foster and Bathmaker 1993).

The issuing of the 1992 orders was not, however, the end of the development of the NCPE at a national 'level'. In 1993, with implementation of the NCPE still in only its early stages, the government announced a forthcoming revision of the National Curriculum as a whole. Revised orders for all subjects were to be produced as a matter of urgency amid ever increasing dissatisfaction within schools at the 'overload' experienced as more National Curriculum subjects 'came on line'. It was now obvious to all (even the Conservative government) that the parts of the National Curriculum did not constitute a coherent or manageable whole. For the NCPE, as for all subjects, this meant that a *reduction* in content was required (Dearing 1993).

The revision of the NCPE: reduction and reinforcement

The need for a revision of the National Curriculum as a whole drew particular attention to three aspects of the policy process identified in Chapter 2: the interaction between policies; between texts and the contexts of their production and implementation; and the arrangements for policy development. The implementation of the NCPE was effectively halted by the government's acknowledgement that in its existing form the National Curriculum was not only unpopular with teachers, but was also fast proving to be unworkable. The government therefore 'invited' Sir Ron Dearing, the chair of the School Curriculum and Assessment Authority (SCAA) to conduct a comprehensive review of the National Curriculum and to make recommendations for its revision.

The shortcomings of many of the arrangements for the development of the National Curriculum were reflected in Dearing's report to the government. Specifically, Dearing stressed that while revision was clearly a matter of urgency, 'getting it right' and, therefore, allowing adequate time to achieve this, was essential. In addition he emphasised the problems of a subject-by-subject approach to development, and thus the need for all subjects to be considered at the same time in a revision. Dearing stated that 'in the opinion of many teachers the combined weight of the National Curriculum is, for the typical teacher teaching a typical class, in excess of the teaching time available' (1993: 30). To ensure both manageability and coherence, he emphasised that the orders must be 'revised together rather than sequentially' (ibid.: 28). A further 'failing' identified by Dearing related to the limited extent to which teachers had been involved in the development of the National Curriculum. He argued that the revision must include teachers and headteachers 'so that the new curricula can be grounded in the realities of the classroom and school planning and management' (ibid.: 39).

In the light of these observations, very different 'arrangements for policy' (Hill 1980) were established for the revision of the National Curriculum. Dearing recommended that all subjects be considered at once and that groups and communication structures were established to facilitate coherency of 'the whole'. In his view advisory groups were needed for each subject, but also key stages. Dearing (1993) stated:

> The key to this whole operation will be co-ordination of these subject advisory groups at each key stage. Key stage groups constituted on the same lines as the subject groups will therefore be established to advise on the educational coherence and manageability of the Orders in the light of the distinctive needs of pupils at each key stage.
>
> (1993: 39)

The need for the membership of the advisory groups to give far greater representation to teachers was also now recognised. In the case of physical education the advisory group included eight 'school representatives' (including teachers and headteachers from both primary and secondary schools), one representative of higher education, a physical education adviser and an advisory teacher from Local Education Authorities, alongside a 'lay person' and representatives of SCAA, the Curriculum Council for Wales (CCW), the Department for Education (DFE) and the Office for Standards in Education (OFSTED).

Although these were significant changes in the policy process, we need to be cautious in equating them with a shift in the relative influence of different players in policy making, and particularly in relations between central government and teachers. In important respects the revision reinforced inequalities in power relations and revealed once again the limits to teachers' influence and authority in the development of the National Curriculum. While the advisory groups included both teachers and headteachers, the degree to which this inclusion signalled an openness on the part of the government and its agencies to listen to their views was certainly questionable. The advisory groups had a very specific task:

> The task ahead is to identify a slimmed down statutory content for each subject, leaving the remainder of the material in the present curriculum Orders for use at the discretion of the school. It will not involve the introduction of new material. Neither will significant changes be made to the structuring of material unless there is a clear need to do so.
>
> (Dearing 1993: 35)

Thus it was made very clear that the revision would *not* entail any rethinking of the overlying structure of the National Curriculum as a whole. Within subjects there were similarly non-negotiable matters. In the case of physical education, this applied not only to the structure of the curriculum, but also the privileging of some areas of activity over others and, specifically, the prominence of games in the NCPE (see the next section). The revision of the NCPE finally showed the government's willingness to use its authority very openly in order to ensure that its discourses would continue to be privileged in the policies and practices of physical education in schools.

Once again, the timescale for policy development was demanding. Dearing (1993) recommended that the new orders should be implemented in September 1995 for all years in key stages 1, 2 and 3. He acknowledged the concerns relating to this schedule for the revision and, specifically, whether or not this would give schools sufficient time to develop new curriculum plans. Nevertheless his view was that there was 'an overwhelming need to relieve teachers of the burden of overload', such that 'it would be quite wrong to perpetuate the current situation for any teacher longer than is absolutely necessary' (Dearing 1993: 72).

Games for all

In the case of physical education, there were limits to the reductions that the advisory group could make to what was already a significantly diminished curriculum. There was, after all, only one attainment target in the NCPE. Once again, therefore, it was the programmes of study that were the focus of attention, and specifically, the areas of activity that schools would be required to include in each of the four key stages. As in all subjects, the pressure and requirement was to cut content.

It was widely acknowledged that the primary curriculum was unmanageable in its present form, with teachers, teacher training, physical resources in schools and the time available for physical education all regarded as inadequate to meet the requirements to address *all* areas of activity. Pragmatic concerns therefore underpinned a move to reduce the number of areas of activity in key stage 1 from five to three. The areas of outdoor and adventurous activities and athletic activities were removed 'allowing schools to concentrate on teaching *Games, Gymnastic Activities* and *Dance*, in order to provide pupils with a foundation of basic movement and understanding' (SCAA 1994a: ii, original emphasis). The additional comments that the programmes of study for dance had been 'amended with an overall reduction in content' and that 'Some elements have been deleted from Gymnastic Activities', while the programme of study for games 'has been clarified a little but no essential content has been removed' (ibid.) indicated once again the influence of political and ideological interests in the policy process. It was apparent that debates within the advisory group had to embrace not only the concerns for a curriculum that was deliverable and manageable in differing school contexts, but also the government's view that sport and specifically traditional games should be the central feature of the physical education curriculum. At this time the government explicitly stated its desire to reinforce this emphasis. *The Times* newspaper quoted a 'leaked' government statement explaining that 'The Government will be taking the opportunity of the revision of the national curriculum further to entrench the position of games within the school curriculum' (Wood 1994). Another newspaper pointed towards the less than subtle intentions of the leak saying that this could well be 'an attempt to push the Department for Education into accepting a more radical plan for reviving sports' (Marston and Jones 1994).

The recommendations for the programmes of study in the other key stages were also seen by some as reflecting the pressures for:

> ... a return to the days of the empire when the school sporting world was divided, for boys at least, into two camps: those who relished rugby, football or whatever, and those who, frozen, were terrified by it but played it anyway.
>
> (Jones 1994)

At key stage 2 there was clearly a tension between the desire for a reduction of content and the maintenance of breadth and balance in the programmes of study. The decision was made to retain all areas in a reduced form. Embraced in the reductions were the political and ideological imperatives to privilege games. It was explained that 'pruning has taken place in all programmes of study but *less so for games*' (SCAA 1994a: ii, our emphasis). This privileging of games was more explicit in the revised recommendations for key stage 3. Again, the advisory group had juggled possibilities as to how to achieve the necessary cut in content. Ultimately SCAA explained that each area of activity *other than games* would be split into two 'half-units'. The requirement for key stage 3 was that pupils study games as a full unit, one other full unit and two half-units from different areas of activity. At least one half-unit was to be either gymnastics or dance. Games was to be pursued in each year of the key stage. Recognising teachers' dissatisfaction with the pattern of pursuing swimming in the context of other areas of activity, swimming was reinstated as an area of activity in its own right (SCAA 1994a). Although SCAA expressed its view that breadth and balance had been 'preserved' in these requirements, as we will see, not all would agree.

The more contentious aspect of the revision of the NCPE related, however, to key stage 4. Here the inequalities in the policy process with regard to the respective authority of the different players in the game became quite explicit. The advisory group *resisted* the political pressures for games also to be a compulsory activity at key stage 4. However, SCAA was unable and/or unwilling to adopt a similar stance and in issuing the draft proposals, instead adhered to the government's desires. They recommended that at least one of the activities experienced at key stage 4 *must* be a game. Once again, established practice provided a convenient justification of the reinforcement of this bias within the NCPE, with SCAA stating that 'The overwhelming majority of pupils, some 90 per cent, participate in a game at this key stage' (ibid.: iii).

In the draft proposals, SCAA had clearly adopted and was openly privileging the government's agenda for physical education. Throughout it was emphasised that games included 'competitive team games'. SCAA also stated that the recommendation for games to be compulsory in key stage 4 'reflects the opportunities that team games provide in promoting team spirit, good sportsmanship, self-discipline, and fair play' (1994a: iii). As on many previous occasions, it was conveniently overlooked that this potential was not unique to team games, nor was there any guarantee in these or other activities that the desired values and attitudes would be those that were expressed and promoted in and through physical education (Evans 1990; Penney and Evans 1994).

The revision of the NCPE did, however, permit another of the established lobby groups within physical education, 'health', to emerge with strengthened representation of its interests, perhaps reflecting that representatives of this lobby were present on the Dearing advisory group and were increasingly proactive in the development of the NCPE. Statements concerning health related exercise were now incorporated in introductory paragraphs for the programmes of study for each key stage and it seemed more likely that teachers would be encouraged to incorporate health issues in units of work. Since the revision of the NCPE this aspect of the requirements has received considerable attention among the physical education profession and a growing body of work addressing the application of health related exercise in curriculum design, lesson plans and delivery has emerged (see for example Almond and Harris 1997; Harris and Elbourn 1992a; 1992b; Harris and Cale 1998).

We WILL dictate the play

Once again the NCPE proposals were the subject of a 'consultation'. SCAA received over 4,000 responses in this process (SCAA 1994b: 44). Although this seemed a weighty response it represented only a small proportion of the number of state schools and teachers who were to implement the NCPE. The scope of the requirements at key stage 2 were regarded as likely to still be too demanding, while 'The compulsory requirement of a competitive game concerned a majority of Key Stage 4 teachers' (ibid.: 45). The Curriculum Council for Wales echoed these concerns, saying that 'In the Council's view, the interests of pupils at this age are best served by giving them an unrestricted choice as to which two activities they choose from the six Areas of Activity' (Plaut, in Awdurod Cwricwlwm Asesu Cymru (ACAC) 1994). Consultation with parents and employers revealed that 'Competitive individual and team games are valued; however, parents do not generally feel that they should be compulsory' (SCAA 1994b: 56).

However, the bottom line was that neither teachers, parents nor the CCW had any authority in the policy process. They could state their opinion and voice opposition, but this could be, and was, ignored by SCAA on behalf of the Conservative government. The requirements for key stage 4 remained as they had been drafted. Some references to '*competitive* games' in key stage 1 were removed in the light of comments at consultation, but the word 'competitive' was retained in the text of the games area of activity at this key stage. For key stage 2, a hierarchy of areas was effectively created in an attempt to reduce the expected coverage of all. It was now stated that pupils should experience games, gymnastic activities and dance in each year of the key stage, and athletic activities, outdoor adventurous activities and swimming 'at points during the key stage' (ibid. 1994b: 45). Following the release of the draft proposals the then Secretary of State for Education, John Patten indicated that, finally, the government had achieved the NCPE text that it desired. He said:

> I am particularly pleased to see the emphasis given to competitive team games in key stages 1–3 of the PE order, and your recommendation that games should be made a requirement at key stage 4 ...
>
> (Patten, in SCAA 1994a)

The extent to which these interests retained their privileged and dominant position in schools' implementation of the NCPE remained to be seen.

Conclusion: flexibility; within frames

The process described in this and the preceding chapter was both complex and openly political. It was a progressive process, in which the NCPE text was *gradually* manipulated and transformed. Critical in this transformation were the 'arrangements for policy' (Hill 1980). Power relations were carried within and by the policy process, the boundaries between policy content and contexts were blurred, and the relationship between content and contexts was always dynamic (see Chapter 2). In this latter respect we note not only the importance of the contemporary economic and political contexts in which the NCPE was developed, but also the historical context of physical education in England and Wales.

The fact that the structure and emphasis of the NCPE mirrored the familiar and established was critical in enabling the government to 'push through' its specific recommendations. As we discuss in Chapter 6, teachers' resistance to this aspect of the development was distinctly limited.

For all the emphasis of 'control' and 'direction' from central government, however, we also need to recall an apparent contradiction within the text of the NCPE. The economic context in which the NCPE was 'made' demanded the production of a 'skeletal' policy (Hill 1980). By its very nature the policy created the capacity for slippage in implementation. The ability of the government to determine what would constitute the NCPE in practice was, to a degree, limited. Furthermore, the ERA, again reflecting the economic and political context of policy development, demanded the active involvement of *other sites* (and particularly LEAs) in the forthcoming implementation of the NCPE. This could be expected to give rise to different forms of policy and further texts, which could variously correspond to or contradict the text produced by central government. Sites and individuals now charged with 'implementation' had, on the surface, the capacity to create 'new' policies; to embed different discourses within the text of the NCPE; to challenge the discourses that it privileged. At the same time, however, there were clear boundaries within which the slippage seemed set to occur. The statutory orders provided a particular definition of physical education that mirrored the definition of the curriculum inherent in the National Curriculum (see Chapter 1) and established practice in physical education in England and Wales. It remained to be seen if the principle of classification (Bernstein 1990, 1996) embedded in these texts could and would be challenged by those charged with implementation. The interaction of structural, discursive, political and economic frames (see Chapter 2) had resulted in the production of a particular policy text. Our attention in the following chapters centres upon how these frames, and new ones emerging in the policy process, influenced implementation and shaped 'new' NCPE texts in particular ways. We investigate how the NCPE texts were received, interpreted and implemented by key players in policy implementation and curriculum development in schools; first LEAs and then schools and teachers within them. In both instances we further illustrate the complexities of the policy process and, in particular, the way in which links between sites in the policy process are critical in the development and implementation of texts, and play a key role in determining the privileging of particular discourses and subordination of others. We show the potential for slippage in the process while also illustrating the way in which particular discourses can be repeatedly reinforced, and that implementation can display important continuities in policy development and thereby sustain an already conservative status quo.

Summary

The government's response to the working group's interim report signalled the start of a change in the emphasis and nature of the NCPE. Pragmatic and ideological concerns were highlighted by the Secretary of State, who demanded significant changes to the NCPE. On the one hand the government called for an increased degree of prescription, specifically in relation to the inclusion of games. On the other, they desired more flexibility and some reduction in requirements, primarily to accommodate differences in school resources for physical education. The opinions of commentators (associations, teachers and others) varied but, ultimately, carried little weight in the debates that followed. The NCPE text was reduced and reshaped, pragmatic concerns were clearly privileged over and above educational interests, and the interests of performance in sport (and particularly games) were given precedence over other areas. This process began with the working group's publication of a final report and continued with the NCC's consultation report and draft orders, the statutory orders published in 1992 and then the revised orders issued in 1995. The revision of the National Curriculum addressed all subjects and recognised the unmanageable and incoherent nature of the curriculum that had been developed between 1989 and 1992. The Dearing Report (1993) outlined the reductions required for the National Curriculum and recommended quite different arrangements for the policy development in the revision. The degree to which teachers had any greater voice in the process was, however, still questionable, and in the context of physical education, the revision was notable for the further explicit privileging of games. Nevertheless, the NCPE remained a policy of clear compromises and tensions, with obvious prescription and yet also some flexibility for different interpretations to emerge in implementation.

Further reading

For further details of the progressive development of the 'official text' of the NCPE, readers should refer to the original texts issued by the government and its aides:

DES and WO (1991) *National Curriculum Physical Education Working Group Interim Report*. London: DES.

DES and WO (1991) *Physical Education for Ages 5–16. Proposals of the Secretary of State for Education and the Secretary of State for Wales*. London: DES.

DES and WO (1992) *Physical Education in the National Curriculum*. London: DES

Department for Education (DFE) and WO (1995) *Physical Education in the National Curriculum*. London: DFE.

The Dearing Report (1993) (Dearing, R. (1993) *The National Curriculum and its Assessment. Final Report*. London: SCAA) provides essential background to the revision of the National Curriculum and the NCPE specifically.

Chapter 5

Controlling the mid-field? Local government in the policy process

In this chapter we centre attention on a critical site of decision making and action in relation to the much debated gap between policy and practice in education; **local government**. Specifically, we address the work of the Local Education Authorities (LEAs) in England and Wales. Historically LEAs and the education advisers who operate within them have been key intermediaries between central government and schools in relation to developments in education. They have often acted as recontextualising agencies (Bernstein 1990; see Chapter 7), fine-tuning central state policies to meet local education and community needs. The ERA policies of local management of schools (LMS) and open enrolment were testimony to the influence that LEAs had enjoyed in education in England and Wales in this respect. Crudely regarding LEAs to be bastions of left wing radicalism and inefficiency, the Conservative government openly sought to reduce LEAs' authority and facilitate a restructuring of the education system in a way that would establish more direct links between central government and schools (see for example, Gerwitz *et al.* 1995; Simon 1988). However, as we will see, after the ERA LEAs remained important intermediaries in the policy process. Although their independence and authority cannot be equated to, for example, the freedom of state and territory governments in Australia (who have been able to adapt, adopt and/or reject the federal 'national' curriculum initiative as they have seen fit, see for example Carter 1995), local government in England and Wales has remained a key point of influence in relation to teachers' interpretations of and responses to central government texts (see also Wallace 1998). Like ourselves Gerwitz *et al.* have stressed that 'it is a mistake to simply "write-off" LEAs as a significant factor in the "planning" of local systems of education' (1995: 57) and have highlighted the importance of local politics, social geographies and histories in shaping and 'distorting' national policy.

This chapter therefore pursues the influences of LEAs in the development of the National Curriculum for Physical Education and in particular, the nature and degree of 'slippage' (Bowe *et al.* 1992) evident at this site in the policy process. We examine both the 'upward' and 'downward' dimensions of the policy process and show that while there was capacity for slippage, there were also limitations to it. We document important elements of continuity between texts produced by local and central government and explore factors underlying and/or prompting this tendency. We address both the direct and more subtle and indirect dimensions of the influence of local government, but also draw attention to some notable constraints to its influence. In addressing these matters we focus attention on interactions between policy texts and the contexts of their development, and between policies. Specifically we examine the ways in which, via their introduction of local management of schools (LMS), LEAs could enhance or constrain curriculum development opportunities in schools' implementation of the NCPE.

Our discussion centres upon the actions and policies of the LEAs that were the focus of our research during the development and subsequent revision of the NCPE (see Appendix A). We stress once again that the responses of these authorities were not necessarily mirrored in other LEAs, but also that many of the issues and processes identified can be expected to feature in arenas of local government. There is evidence to suggest that many of the shortcomings that we highlight in the implementation of the NCPE and that we link to LEA policies and support (such as the maintenance of facilities for physical education and the loss of physical education time for study of a second language) are characteristics far from unique to the LEAs that we have studied, and, furthermore, are outstanding concerns in the implementation of the NCPE (see for example Clay 1997a, 1997b). To retain the anonymity of the authorities who enabled us access, the referencing of documents issued by them has necessarily been amended. The LEA documents that we refer to are listed in Appendix B rather than in the main bibliography.

Roles and responsibilities in the development of the National Curriculum

LEAs had two key roles to play in the development of the National Curriculum. First, the arrangements for policy were such that dissemination of and consultation on the texts being developed nationally was invariably via LEAs. Second, the ERA identified LEAs as responsible for overseeing and supporting the successful implementation of the National Curriculum in schools within their authority (DES 1989a). It was LEAs rather than central government that had the responsibility for ensuring that schools fulfilled their legal obligation to provide all children with the National Curriculum that was now their entitlement, and it was LEAs who schools looked to for support and advice in implementation. Inevitably, therefore, they represented a site in which policy would be interpreted and, to varying degrees, adapted in the light of local economic and political contexts and interests, and where 'new' or 'hybrid' policies would be produced (see Chapter 2). Potentially local government was an arena in which discourses could be contested, new discourses embedded and/or privileged in texts and in which significant slippage could occur.

'Consultation' and representation

LEAs were charged with co-ordinating teachers' responses to key policy texts in the development of the NCPE. Although teachers could always make a direct response in the National Curriculum consultations, in the development of the NCPE much of the feedback from teachers was subject to interpretation and editing by LEAs. Our account of these processes within one LEA, which we call Seashire, serves to illustrate several important features of the policy process. The primary focus for our discussion is the formulation of Seashire's response to the interim report from the NCPE working group (DES and WO 1991a; see Chapter 3) 'on behalf of' the teachers within its authority. As we will see, our data point to the marginal and subordinate role of teachers in the development of the curriculum that they were legally bound to deliver. It is notable that we are dealing here with the 'upward flow' in the policy process; the transmission of teachers' texts to the arena of central government. As we will see, these transmissions, as those *from* central government *to* teachers, involved the creation of multiple (and hybrid) texts. This upward flow therefore also had inherent scope for slippage between sites and we saw the potential for policy to be *transformed* in its transmission. Below we show the way in which both the national texts received by teachers, and their own responses to these, were the subject of interpretation and alteration by representatives of LEAs.

Formulating a 'teachers' response' to the NCPE

The publication of the interim report provided the first opportunity for teachers to comment on the development of the NCPE. The feedback given to the working group was clearly critical in relation to the direction that the subsequent development of the NCPE would take. The physical education inspectors in Seashire sought to collate written responses from teachers, but also chose to hold two 'National Curriculum response days' to facilitate discussion of the interim report and to provide a time efficient means of gathering feedback from teachers within the authority. Physical education teachers, physical education co-ordinators or other relevant staff from all primary and secondary schools were invited to attend one of the two days. Our own attendance of one of these days showed that there were important inequalities inherent in the policy process in terms of the differing capacity of individuals to 'speak' and 'be heard'. Teachers were certainly not in a position of authority in this consultation exercise.

Few teachers had seen the interim report prior to attending the response days. Others had obtained a copy but had not had time to examine it amid the demands of their busy everyday lives. By virtue of the 'arrangements for policy' (Hill 1980) teachers were therefore heavily reliant on the interpretation of the interim report that they were presented with by the LEA's physical education inspectors and this was both selective and far from neutral. Teachers were introduced to what, in the views of the LEA physical education inspectors, constituted the 'issues arising' from the interim report and presented with opinions about these issues. In addressing matters such as the attainment targets for physical education (see Chapter 3), the requirements for key stage 4, the language used in the report, and the requirements for swimming, the inspectors expressed their clear support for the NCPE working group and open opposition to the views expressed by the Secretary of State. The Secretary of State's letter of response to the working group was described as 'dismissive' and one of the LEA inspectors went as far as to say that 'at the end of the day' they [the inspectors] wanted to be able to say that the response from the teachers within the authority was 'loudly and clearly in support of the document, and loudly and clearly for getting rid of Kenneth Clarke [the Secretary of State for Education]' (LEA PE Inspector, cited in Penney 1994: 132).

The 'consultation' day clearly revealed that the different positions of individuals and groups with respect to their access to information was crucial in terms of the role that they were able to play in the policy process. Although one of the inspectors stressed that the teachers should feel free to discuss issues other than those presented to them, the views that had been expressed and the structure provided for discussions unavoidably shaped the debates that followed. The issues to be considered had essentially been defined as offering teachers a simple choice; to support the working group and its proposals, or to support the Secretary of State's views. Furthermore, the 'choice' that teachers were expected to make had already been stated (Penney 1994). However, the teachers present demonstrated their capacity, at least to some degree, to deviate from the LEA's directive text. They drew particular attention to their concerns about the practicalities and resource implications of the proposed recommendations, particularly in primary schools. While the majority of teachers appeared to appreciate the work done by the working group in producing the interim report and saw value in the proposals, many also had concerns about the prospects of implementation. Significantly, no such doubts were expressed in the 'official text' of the LEA's 'teachers' response'. The 'official response' from the LEA 'on behalf' of teachers within the authority was written by one of the LEA's physical education inspectors and its production vividly demonstrated the significance of the arrangements for policy. The text seemed to reflect the inspectors' belief that a clear message of support for the proposals was what was required if the proposals outlined in the interim report (and therefore a worthwhile NCPE) were to 'survive'. On the surface at least the LEA seemed driven by educational and political interests rather than teachers' more pragmatic concerns. The authority of writers in the policy process, and the subordinate position of teachers in the development of the NCPE, was very apparent.

As well as omitting reference to teachers' pragmatic concerns, the LEA text was also notable in presenting a picture of a clear consensus of opinion about the issues addressed. Essentially teachers within the authority were portrayed as a homogeneous group with common and agreed views in relation to the development of the NCPE. It was stated that '[Seashire's] teachers strongly support' several of the matters addressed in the Secretary of State's response to the interim report, including 'the need for retaining three attainment targets' and 'the inclusion of swimming' in the NCPE (LEA 1991b; see Penney 1994). The reality was that teachers within the LEA had many, varied and often conflicting interests and at the National Curriculum response day, failed to reach agreement on several issues, such as the inclusion of dance and outdoor education in key stage 3. Clearly the inspectors felt that such diversity had to be overlooked and hidden if certain core principles of educational progressivism were to be protected in the NCPE. Hence we saw in the LEA's 'official text' the expression of solidarity and a more powerful, if artificial, politically expedient view.

The LEA's response also illustrated the potential for *new* discourses to come into play in the policy process. Specifically, the LEA took the opportunity of the response to draw attention to local developments in physical education that it considered relevant to the development of the NCPE. In particular the LEA outlined the 'partnership' that it had established with the regional Sports Council[1] for the joint development and resourcing of programmes seeking to establish closer links between school sport and community based junior sports clubs (including in particular the development of 'Champion Coaching'[2] schemes). The LEA appeared keen to

---

1   The Sports Council was a public body accountable to and receiving funding from central government. It was established in 1972 and had ten regional offices in England, who promoted and delivered policy in partnership with local authorities and other sports organisations. In 1996 the Sports Council was replaced by two new bodies, the UK Sports Council and the English Sports Council. Both receive funding and are accountable to the Department of Culture, Media and Sport. The English Sports Council has retained regional offices.

2   Champion Coaching was a national initiative developed by the National Coaching Foundation that sought to bring together different agencies to develop coaching for school age children after school hours and to provide coach education for those working with these children (see DES and WO 1991b; Walsh 1992).

be seen to be proactive and innovative, and to gain recognition as a site of 'good practice' in physical education and sport. We can also note, however, that these initiatives legitimated the central government's focus upon sport over and above physical education. We can see a tension between such apparent compatibility of the LEA's and central government's direction in developments, and the elements of resistance and opposition on the part of the LEA that we noted earlier.

In mediating the teachers' texts in these ways the LEA had indicated its position as an influential intermediary in policy and curriculum development in education. It had also provided an important insight into aspects of and inequalities in the policy process that were certainly not unique to this LEA, nor this development. Similar patterns of involvement and influence were observed in a different LEA when the National Curriculum was revised in 1994 (see Appendix A). For example, at a day conference held to gather teachers' responses to the draft proposals for the revised NCPE, teachers received a 'reduced' and modified version of the national text and, once again, many teachers struggled to formulate opinions about proposals that they were seeing for the first time. Again we saw the privileged position of the LEA and subordinate position of teachers. We can also reflect upon other instances in which such positionings and 'slippage' are likely to feature in policy developments. The consultation conducted by various professional associations and organisations (see Chapter 4) needs to be viewed in a similar light. The writers of 'organisations' responses' to the various NCPE texts can also be seen as occupying a privileged position in the policy process.

Playing the same game

The discussion above has emphasised the 'hybrid' nature of the text that the LEA presented to teachers in the development of the NCPE. However, we also need to address compatibilities between the LEA's text and that produced by central government. While contestation certainly featured in consultation, there was nevertheless relatively little deviation from the agenda established by central government. Effectively, the progressively narrowing agenda in the development of the NCPE was further reinforced and legitimated by LEAs. LEAs lacked the scope, power and desire to bring new issues to the forefront of debates, to question matters such as the structure that was being adopted as the framework for defining and developing the curriculum, or how matters such as equal opportunities were to be expressed within the programmes of study. Certainly, LEAs appeared to be operating within distinct and constraining discursive frames in which both political and economic agendas were embedded.

'Support', 'advice' and 'direction' in implementation

LEA PE advisers and/or inspectors (see p. 85) represented a critical source of advice for teachers now facing the task of implementing the NCPE. In this role they presented clear evidence of the potential for further slippage in the policy process and, furthermore, for *personal* as well as 'official' views and interests to come into play. At the same time, however, we also saw limits to the LEA's influence in the policy process and gained an insight into the critical role that individual schools would play in determining what children received as their NCPE (see Chapter 6).

The 'resistance' to central government policy that Seashire's PE inspectors had displayed in their reading of the interim report also featured in the 'advice' and 'support' that they provided for implementation of the NCPE orders in 1992. Teachers were actively encouraged to refer to the earlier, more extensive and arguably progressive NCPE texts, and particularly the working group's final report. In addition, the physical education inspectors recognised and attempted to fill 'gaps' or omissions in the text of the NCPE, and thereby further shape its 'implementation' in schools. For example, the NCPE could not specify the curriculum time that should be allocated to physical education in schools. 'Advice' from LEAs on this matter would not be prescriptive, but a policy statement could clearly be either used or interpreted by teachers and headteachers as 'official' guidance that should be adhered to. Seashire produced a statement of policy on timetabling for key stage 3, detailing the hours that all its subject inspectors agreed should be allocated to curriculum subjects during the key stage. In an outline totalling 2,790 hours, the recommendation was that 240 hours (8.6 per cent) should be allocated to physical education. The document also drew attention to the need for schools to consider not merely the *total* time allocated but also the *'regularity* and *frequency* with which a subject was "visited"' and the *'size* of the time block' allocated (LEA 1991c: 3, cited in Penney 1994: 198, our emphasis). With respect to the latter concern, the LEA specifically stated:

> In general, time blocks as small as 35 minutes will not be suitable. On the other hand, inspectors are doubtful whether full value is obtained in all subjects when 70 minute lessons are the norm, although these, or longer periods, are valuable for some learning activities.
> (LEA 1991c: 3, ibid.)

There was clear recognition, therefore, that the time allocation for physical education, and its timetabling had important implications for the opportunities that schools were able to provide in the context of their delivery of the NCPE (see Chapter 6). At an in-service training course held to address the implementation of the NCPE, Seashire's inspectors explained that if a 'minimalist view' was adopted in the implementation of the NCPE, the requirement to fulfil programmes of study in only two activities in key stage 4 (see Chapter 4) could be met in a single year, with the prospect of no physical education in year 11. They also identified the timetabling of physical education 'against' a second language as contradictory to the entitlement of all pupils to the NCPE (Penney 1994; see also Chapter 6).

The LEA PE inspectors also went on to address the issue of how curriculum time should be allocated between different activities in physical education. In contrast to the central government's texts they stressed the need for balance to be directly reflected in the time devoted to different activities within the physical education curriculum. The inspectors explained that teachers would need to review their physical education curricula to redress the present games bias that they saw in many programmes (Penney 1994). As we indicated in Chapter 4, others (and particularly those involved in the development of Welsh texts for the NCPE, see CCW 1992, 1994a, 1994b) similarly endeavoured to encourage teachers to temper the dominance of games teaching in their curricula.

Thus, in a number of respects the inspectors and the LEA could be regarded as an important and to some extent oppositional voice in the implementation of the NCPE, tempering the narrowing restorationist aspirations of the Conservative New Right. However, Seashire LEA could do no more than offer *advice*, that ultimately schools and teachers could adopt or reject as they saw fit, albeit within the frame set by the requirements of the NCPE. Furthermore, there were aspects of the advice offered that legitimated and reinforced central government's discourse. In this respect we saw once again the way in which policies were shaped or framed by the contexts and conditions of their making and implementation, and the dynamic nature of the relationship between policy texts and contexts. Located in an intermediary position, LEAs were subject to influences from above, below and around, as well as themselves having an active influence on all of these contexts.

Accountability bites: evidence of implementation

As overseers of the implementation of the National Curriculum, LEAs were also deemed to be to some extent accountable for the success or failure of schools to meet the statutory requirements. In Seashire there was growing concern that schools should produce adequate 'evidence' of 'successful implementation'. This became the focus of in-service courses addressing the implementation of the NCPE. What the LEA inspectors promoted as the 'evidence required' then shaped teachers' focus and priorities in implementation. For the inspectors, the critical matters were not the changes in curriculum design and pedagogies that teachers initiate, but, rather, the representation of these changes expressed in the *administrative aspects* of implementation of the NCPE. The inspectors stressed the need for physical education departments to establish comprehensive curriculum outlines, statements of departmental aims, units and schemes of work, all cross-referenced to the statutory orders for the NCPE. They stressed that this documentation would be the central focus in future government inspections seeking to assess their implementation of the NCPE. The inspectors were anxious that all the necessary paperwork to accompany the introduction of the NCPE should be in place in all departments within Seashire by September 1992. The message that teachers thus received from the inspectorate was that their immediate task in the implementation of the NCPE was the writing of policy texts (Penney 1994). Teachers' fears that the NCPE would 'arrive' with an administrative burden attached (see Chapter 6) were thus confirmed, heralding the prospect of further 'new' and hybrid texts emerging in the policy process.

Appreciating the unpopularity of their expectations, the inspectors went to some lengths to play down the administrative work (and critically, the *changes* to existing policy) involved in implementation. In taking this stance the inspectors gave little encouragement for innovative activity in the design of physical education curricula. One of the inspectors went as far as to say that 'the National Curriculum aims are exactly the same as ours . . . it's not asking you to do anything different' (LEA PE inspector, cited in Penney 1994: 201). Existing documentation therefore needed 'sharpening . . . we need to make it National Curriculum proof' (ibid.). In addition, the inspectors drew attention to the fact that in the first year of implementation the NCPE *only* had to be introduced for the *first year* of key stages 1, 2 and 3. Their advice to departments in secondary schools was therefore that they *only* address their year 7 curriculum, and produce the necessary documentation to accompany this, then the following year, do likewise for year 8, thus adopting a 'rolling programme' approach to implementation (Penney 1994). This overlooked that a 'rolling programme' could (at least in the short term) discourage curriculum planning for the key stage as a whole, and thereby jeopardise the development of continuity and progression in curriculum design. Again pragmatic interests prevailed over educational considerations.

In the following chapter we examine school responses to the NCPE in the light of the advice offered by the LEA inspectors and the ways in which teachers' texts were shaped or framed by this advice. First, however, we remind readers of the significance of not only what was included in the LEA texts, but also what was omitted. There was little encouragement to consider alternative organisational structures that might be developed in implementing the curriculum, or any insight into how permeating themes could be promoted in design and delivery, or the teaching methods and grouping strategies that should be employed. By emphasising technical and pragmatic rather than educational conside-rations, Seashire further consolidated rather than checked the momentum towards the reproduction of the status quo in the practices of physical education.

We now turn attention to some of the more indirect influences of LEA policies in the development of the NCPE. In particular we highlight that inherent in LEAs' policies were similar tensions and apparent contradic-tions to those identified in the ERA itself; most notably between the National Curriculum commitment to 'entitlement for all' and the parallel introduction of market principles to education. In Chapter 1 we explained that the ERA required each LEA to develop its own LMS scheme and, following the government's approval of their scheme, to introduce it within their authority. We also indicated the requirement for all schemes to develop 'formula funding' with the criteria of the number and age of pupils as the basis for allocating the majority of funds to individual schools. LEAs identified budget items to be excluded from formula funding as 'discretionary exceptions' (see DES 1988) and detailed their formulas for allocating the remaining funds to schools. This demanded that they specify an amount to be paid per pupil in each year of schooling for numerous individual budget items. In studying the detail and implementation of the LMS scheme in Seashire we saw very clearly that 'the overall operational framework of the school market . . . offers only a very crude sense of the workings and effects of specific local education markets' (Gerwitz *et al.* 1995: 57) and that the diversities and idiosyncrasies of local settings means that we cannot generalise about the precise nature and effects of market forces in education (ibid.). These matters of differences within the educa-tion system after the ERA and the importance of local contexts and influences in implementation of nationally derived policy are ones that we also address in Chapter 6, where our focus is on individual schools, the curricula and teachers within them.

Flaws in funding

The move to formula funding had notable implications for the funding and resourcing of physical education and, therefore, schools' abilities to successfully implement the NCPE and provide *all* pupils with the curriculum that was their legal entitlement. Below we highlight several ways in which these implications were evident in Seashire and thus point to the significance of LEAs as sites of the mediation and 'refraction' of the legislative framework set by central government (Gerwitz *et al.* 1995).

In Seashire there was a clear commitment to *maximise* the proportion of funds allocated on the formula basis. When LMS was introduced the

Conservative government stated that it expected all LEAs to restrict their spending on discretionary exceptions to 10 per cent of their general schools budget (GSB) and then aim to reduce this element to 7 per cent of that budget (see DES 1988). In 1990 Seashire proudly announced that:

> ... in the first year of formula funding [Seashire] was in the top ten of LEAs giving the largest proportion of budgets to schools. Before April 1993 [Seashire] is committed to delegating substantially more of the discretionary elements.
>
> (LEA 1990a: 3, cited in Penney 1994: 172)

This stance ultimately detracted from the LEA's ability to manage and therefore meet the *different* financial needs of schools within its authority.

With respect to **facilities**, DES *Circular No. 7/88* stated that the Secretary of State's expectation was that the costs of 'day-to-day internal maintenance', 'minor emergency repairs' and grounds maintenance would be delegated. A suggested division of responsibilities between LEAs and schools for repairs and maintenance was also provided (DES 1988). Seashire delegated funding for non-structural repairs and maintenance, with floor area being identified as a factor in the formula allocation for this item. Significantly, the LEA also incorporated a 'condition factor' into its calculations, recognising that variations in the age and condition of facilities would have different implications for repair and maintenance costs. Internal decoration and maintenance, including, for example, the upkeep of gymnasium floors, was also delegated. While the funding arising from these arrangements was adequate for minor repairs and maintenance, it seemed highly questionable whether schools would be able to undertake major repairs that would inevitably be required some time in the future. One headteacher in the authority explained that he faced the 'problem of how to find £20,000 to refloor a sports hall' (Headteacher, cited in Penney 1994: 236).

In the case of school based **swimming pools**, the LEA acknowledged that difficulties could arise with delegated funding. It explained that where pools were provided as a recognised teaching space (a status it accorded following assessment of other facilities on the school site and pupil numbers), funds for maintenance would be allocated on a school specific basis, but that in other cases, funding would only be on this basis until the end of the transitional period for LEAs' introduction of LMS;[3] i.e. 3 March 1993. Seashire stated that thereafter school governors would 'have to accept financial responsibility or discontinue use of the pool' (LEA 1990b: 9, cited in

---

3   LEAs could have a phased introduction of some aspects of their LMS scheme, with transitional arrangements to be phased out by 1994 (see DES, 1988).

Penney 1994: 177). This clause of Seashire's LMS scheme had important implications not only for all schools with on-site swimming pools, but also many others using these facilities. In Seashire there were 300 primary schools; 57 of these schools used their own pools for swimming provision and a further 95 used pools at other schools (Penney 1994). Effectively the LEA was delegating the 'burden' of swimming pool upkeep to schools and was clearly placing some schools in a position of having to decide whether or not they would be able to finance continued usage of their pools. One head of physical education said 'Once LMS becomes fully implemented I am concerned as to who pays for our swimming pool maintenance. We may not be able to fund it' (cited in Penney 1994: 236).

The prospect of the closure of some pools highlighted inherent inadequacies of delegated funding and was clearly a worrying potential outcome of the introduction of LMS. In Seashire it was also somewhat ironic, as the LEA had historically demonstrated a clear commitment to the provision of swimming in the physical education curriculum. Before the move to LMS the LEA had developed a county swimming programme in which the provision of fifteen 30-minute swimming sessions (or equivalent) was a 'basic entitlement' for all year 5 pupils. At a glance, Seashire's LMS scheme appeared to provide continued support for this entitlement. Specific funding for swimming was incorporated into the formula, with the allocation related to the number of pupils in years 4 and 5. In a letter to headteachers, Seashire's county general inspector (CGI) for PE explained that 'The formula allocates a sum of money (£4.52) in Year 4 and Year 5, giving you the flexibility to provide swimming for your pupils in either of those two years' (cited in Penney 1994: 186). What became apparent, however, were the limitations to this 'flexibility' and, specifically, the way in which formula based funding failed to acknowledge or accommodate the *different* costs that schools faced in providing swimming for their pupils. For schools with a pool on site and/or a qualified swimming teacher on their staff, the allocation was likely to be adequate, but for schools incurring costs of travel to off-site pools, pool hire and swimming instructor fees, the formula driven allocation was clearly inadequate. Ultimately, the CGI for PE was forced to admit that there was a need for the LEA to consider whether it was:

> ... prepared to CHANGE the basis of Swimming fund devolution, and make arrangements to provide funds on an 'earmarked' specific basis to schools. ... The formula funding system does not have sufficient flexibility to meet a site specific swimming programme.
> (LEA CGI for PE, cited in Penney 1994: 188)

Grounds maintenance similarly demonstrated the inappropriateness of formula-based funding for some budget items in education. Differences in the size of school grounds and in pupil numbers meant that with funding on a per capita basis, some schools with a small roll and relatively large grounds faced a major deficit on this budget item, while others with relatively small grounds and a large roll made a substantial profit. Seashire decided to identify a minimum value for grounds maintenance allocations, with schools receiving a supplement if, with per capita funding, the allocation fell below the minimum. Schools that were identified as having a 'site deficiency' also received funds to assist in making alternative provision elsewhere (LEA 1990b, cited in Penney 1994: 178). The need for these arrangements thus highlighted once again that funding on a per capita basis could not accommodate specific needs and situations.

Meanwhile the delegation of funding for **equipment repair and maintenance** had a two-fold impact. On the one hand the ability of these arrangements to cover the costs of the repair and replacement of major items of equipment (such as trampolines, or sets of gymnastics mats) seemed highly questionable. It appeared quite possible that schools may in the future face a situation in which they lacked the equipment required to meet the requirements of the NCPE. In addition, delegation of this funding removed a critical dimension of control that the LEA inspectors had previously enjoyed in relation to ensuring the quality and safety of physical education equipment in schools. Their obvious concern was that desires or needs to save money may see safety jeopardised in physical education.

As well as impacting upon schools, however, the introduction of LMS had important implications for the authority itself and the work of the inspectors within it. Below we discuss ways in which the work of LEAs and, in particular their inspection, advisory and support services fundamentally changed after the ERA, and point to implications of the changes for schools and teachers due to implement the NCPE.

Bidding for business in the education market

Following the ERA, LEAs faced both a reduction in their resources and very different emphases in their work with schools. The devolution of funds to schools left LEAs without the capacity to maintain existing complements of school support staff and changed the nature of the work undertaken by those staff remaining. Essentially, there was a shift to a customer–client relationship between LEAs and schools. After the ERA the survival of the LEA was reliant upon schools choosing to remain within their authority rather than 'opting out' and becoming grant maintained (see Chapter 1) and, furthermore, then commissioning LEA services. LEAs were in a position of having to actively market the support services that they had once provided as a matter of course to schools and teachers within their authority (see also Wallace 1998).

On the surface, giving schools the freedom to choose whether or not they wished to buy into, for example, LEA provision of in-service training for teachers, seemed to give schools greater potential to efficiently identify and then meet teachers' needs. However, as we discuss further in Chapter 6, there were limits to this freedom and critical differences between schools in terms of their ability to 'choose' to provide training for staff. Under Seashire's LMS scheme, funding for both attendance of training courses and the supply teaching (i.e. the provision of a replacement teacher) that may be required to enable that attendance, came from individual school budgets. In this context, attendance was a luxury that not all schools could afford. Furthermore, attendance of training courses was essentially a matter of competition between staff (and departments) within schools. Inevitably, the low status of physical education in many schools and its late arrival in the National Curriculum acted to disadvantage some physical education teachers in their claim for a share of school resources and opportunities for professional development (Penney 1994; see also Chapter 6).

The education market of the 1990s was also one in which LEAs clearly lacked adequate resources to provide services desirable to support curriculum development in schools. Seashire was certainly fortunate in retaining the number of inspectors that it did. Elsewhere in England and Wales cost saving cuts in staffing meant that some authorities were left with *no* physical education inspectors, advisers or advisory teachers. In other authorities it was left to a solitary inspector to attempt to undertake the workload that had previously been deemed to justify the employment of a team. Even with four physical education inspectors, Seashire struggled to provide the support needed by schools and teachers facing implementation of the NCPE. Significantly, it became increasingly evident that the provision of *support* was no longer a justifiable priority for the inspectors. They faced pressures to adopt the Conservative government's stance that *inspection* rather than *advice*, was to be the key means of achieving improved standards in schools. These pressures and the shift in focus within LEAs and in its relations with schools and teachers was particularly evident after the Schools Act of 1992. This Act abolished Her Majesty's Inspectorate (HMI) that had previously undertaken school inspections for the government and established an Office for Standards in Education (OFSTED), a non-ministerial government department, to contract teams of inspectors to undertake school inspections. Seashire, like many other LEAs, submitted a bid to carry out the inspections within the schools in its authority. The success of this bid was critical in securing the inspectors' jobs and ensuring the future solvency of the authority, but it also created problems for them. On the one hand the time to be devoted to inspections was considerable and their clear priority. On the other, their identification as OFSTED inspectors could inhibit the development of supportive relations with schools and teachers within them. Inspections were clearly perceived as a threat and an ordeal for schools, and it was thus questionable whether the roles of inspection and support were any longer compatible (see also Evans and Penney 1994). In several other authorities we saw similar pressures for officers to devote time and energy to inspections rather than to the provision of support and advice to teachers. Economically as well as discursively, the inspection, advisory and support activities of the LEA were thus clearly framed by the conditions they were operating in after the ERA.

A further characteristic of these conditions was that LEAs were no longer the *sole* suppliers of certain services, such as grounds maintenance. Under LMS schools had the choice of whether to remain within the authority's central contract for these services or make their own independent arrangements. With its own future existence at stake, we saw Seashire adopt a market discourse to promote the grounds maintenance and the transport service that it would now be offering to its 'clients'. With respect to the transport service, it was stressed that with Seashire's central control, 'quality control' would be assured, only 'reputable operators' would be used and 'problems regarding poor performance by the contractor will be dealt with by me as part of this comprehensive service arrangement' (LEA County Surveyor, cited in Penney 1994: 179).

While emphasising the way in which the actions of the LEA and the discourses that it privileged reflected and were shaped by those surrounding it, it is inaccurate, however, to portray local government as a passive player in the policy process. Indeed, Wallace has particularly highlighted the ability of LEAs to develop what he terms 'counter-policies' that 'reflected neither the practices envisaged by ministers nor the spirit of their reforms' (1998: 196). Thus the *political* stance taken by the authority and the *specific* policies that it then developed were themselves critical in the creation of particular conditions within the authority and in its schools. Not all authorities had the same allegiances or followed the same path in their development of LMS and implementation of the National Curriculum. In particular, authorities varied in the degree to which they were committed to maximising the delegation of funds and, inevitably, in their degree of interest in and support for physical education. In Seashire there was evidence of an inherent tension between a commitment to the entitlement of all to the National Curriculum and the parallel promotion of market values in education. As we see below, Seashire's response to further issues arising from the ERA reaffirmed these tensions.

Paying to play

The ERA presented schools with the opportunity to retain money generated from use of their facilities outside of school hours. Seashire indicated its clear support for initiatives aimed at developing such use of school facilities, with school sports facilities an obvious focus of attention. However, here again the LEA mediated the influence of the 'market discourse' and attempted to bring other interests into play in policy development. Potentially, the development of community use of facilities (see Chapter 1) posed a threat to pupil access. Extra-curricular physical education activities may either be sacrificed to make way for income-generating community activities, or themselves be subject to a charge. LEAs' advice on these issues was not prescriptive, but could again prove critical in determining school policies. Seashire therefore urged head-teachers to ensure that pupils had free access to the school facilities at lunchtimes and after school. At a conference held to address community use, the CGI for PE expressed his hope that headteachers would 'accept that pupils have free access to the school facilities and that lunchtime and post-school activities should therefore be free' (LEA CGI for PE, cited in Penney 1994: 183). Once again, however, the LEA could only appeal for others to adopt its own stance. It would be for schools and specifically their governing bodies and headteachers to respond as they saw fit (see Chapter 6).

The LEA faced a similar situation in relation to the matter of schools charging pupils for participation in certain activities. The ERA prevented schools meeting costs incurred in activities that were part of the National Curriculum by charging for these activities. However, activities that were not related to the National Curriculum were defined as 'optional extras' and could be subject to a charge. Furthermore, it was stipulated that schools could request 'voluntary contributions' for curricular and extra-curricular activities. Both LEAs and school governing bodies were required to draw up and review their charging policies (DES 1989b). *Circular No. 2/89* explained that:

> There is no legal requirement for LEAs to produce their policies in advance of schools, though in practice schools may want to see the LEA's statement before drawing up their own. The charging and remissions policies adopted by a school governing body may be more or less generous than the policies of the LEA, provided they meet the requirements of the law.
>
> (DES 1989b: 11)

Once again, the indication was that while not prescriptive, LEAs' policies would be significant in determining school policies. In Seashire the County

Education Officer certainly anticipated such influence. Pre-empting the LEA's formal policy statement, he detailed Seashire's stance on this matter. He stated,

> Voluntary contributions from parents should be seen as the normal method of funding activities, including educational visits, which are considered valuable and which the school is unable otherwise to fund. This could apply to the costs of travel, entry to off-site facilities and materials for cookery ...
>
> (LEA County Education Officer, cited in Penney 1994: 184)

As indicated, Seashire had signalled its opposition to schools charging for extra-curricular PE activities. However, the distinction between 'charging' and 'voluntary contributions' was certainly unclear and use of the latter seemed equally likely to produce inequalities in provision and opportunities. Although *Circular No. 2/89* specified that voluntary contributions must be 'genuinely voluntary' and that pupils could not be treated differentially according to whether or not their parents contributed, it stated that an accompanying letter to parents could indicate 'the contribution per pupil which would be required if the activity were to take place' and 'that the activity would not take place if parents were reluctant to support it' (DES 1989b: 12). As the County Education Officer observed 'Parents could argue that a contribution sought in those terms was not voluntary' (LEA County Education Officer, cited in Penney 1994: 185). However, rather than dissuading schools from requesting voluntary contributions, he advised them to be more subtle in their requests:

> It would be better to put to parents that while some trips could take place even if parents of participating children declined to contribute, any trend of that kind would leave the Governing Body with no option but to reduce the pattern of activities.
>
> (Ibid.)

These moves thus again pointed to basic inadequacies in the funding to schools under LMS. Physical education was clearly one of the subjects where the effects of these policies would be felt. In physical education there was a heavy reliance on voluntary contributions, particularly for transport to and entrance charges for community (off-site) facilities (see Chapter 6). Neither the text of the ERA nor that of the LEA acknowledged that different schools would, by virtue of socio-economic differences in their catchment areas, be very differently placed with respect to their ability to generate income by appealing for 'voluntary' contributions. The implications of these differences were in sharp contrast to the commitment to the provision of a broad and balanced physical education curriculum for *all* pupils that the LEA physical education inspectors, reflecting the rhetoric of the National Curriculum, had portrayed in other instances.

Conclusion

Both the LEA's LMS scheme and the policies and actions of its inspection, advisory and support service for physical education set particular economic and discursive frames for the implementation of the NCPE. In LEAs' responses to and implementation of the ERA there was clearly the capacity for the emphases inherent in the policies of central government, and their effects, to be either supported and exacerbated, or interrupted and modified (Gerwitz *et al.* 1995). However, while certainly influential, LEAs were by no means guaranteed a determining role in the development of the NCPE. LEAs' policies and actions were themselves framed by preceding events and surrounding contexts, and furthermore, many decisions crucial to the future provision of physical education and sport in schools would be taken in schools. Headteachers would be key figures in the interpretation of and response to texts issued by both central and local government, and clearly, there was the scope for further slippage in the policy process. In the following chapter we examine schools' and teachers' responses to these texts and address the critical matters of how these texts were expressed in practice, what children in different schools experienced as a NCPE, and the key factors determining the nature of their experiences.

Summary

Local government stands between the policies and actions of central government and schools and as such is an important and influential site in policy and curriculum development in education. In England and Wales Local Education Authorities (LEAs) had both direct and indirect influences in the development and implementation of the National Curriculum. They were responsible for dissemination of and consultation upon central government proposals and then for overseeing and supporting implementation. In addition, via their development in particular of their local management of schools policy, they could shape the opportunities and constraints arising when schools attempted to implement the National Curriculum. LEAs in England and Wales thus held a position of power in that they were charged with relaying policy both from central government to schools, and from teachers to central government. In this process they had the capacity to adapt and modify policy, to bring particular interests to the fore. Equally, however, their actions were constrained by the conditions and demands that the ERA created for them, and by the discursive frames already established for the development of the National Curriculum for Physical Education (NCPE). They also faced a situation in which their own texts and recommendations could ultimately be reshaped and potentially adapted and/or resisted by schools within their authority. LEAs' position in relation to policy and curriculum development was thus one in which their influence was notable but inevitably compromised. Their actions were important in shaping the ongoing development of the NCPE and setting particular frames for its implementation in schools, but there was also scope for further slippage in schools' responses to and implementation of polices issued by central and local government.

Further reading

For further details of local management of schools readers should refer to the:

DES (1988) 'E.R.A.: L.M.S.' *Circular No. 7/88* London: DES.

and/or texts addressing this and other dimensions of the ERA, such as:

Maclure, S. (1989) *Education Re-formed*. London: Hodder & Stoughton.
The LMS Initiative (1990) (2nd edn) *Local Management in Schools: A Practical Guide*. London: The Local Management in Schools Initiative.

Gerwitz, S., Ball, S.J. and Bowe, R. (1995) *Markets, Choice and Equity in Education*. Buckingham: Open University Press, provides an analysis of the implementation and effects of the 'education market' in both LEA and school settings.

Chapters by Jennifer Whisker and Bill Lahr in Barber, M. and Graham, D. (eds) (1993) *Sense and Nonsense in the National Curriculum*. London: Falmer Press, respectively address the implementation of the National Curriculum from an LEA perspective, and provision of training for implementation.

Wyatt, J. (1993) 'Delivering the National Curriculum – An L.E.A. Perspective', *The Bulletin of Physical Education* 29(1): 12–14.

and our own article:

Evans, J. and Penney, D. (1994) 'Whatever Happened to Good Advice? Service and Inspection after the Education Reform Act', *British Educational Research Journal* 20(5): 519–533.

also provide further description and analysis of inspection and advisory services for physical education in the light of the ERA and subsequent policies issued by central government.

Chapter 6

Policy in practice

In this chapter we centre attention on the roles and influences of **physical education teachers** in policy and curriculum development and, in particular, in the development and implementation of the National Curriculum for Physical Education (NCPE) in England and Wales. In our continuing analysis of this policy process, we explore the relative influences of central and local government texts, school and surrounding contexts on teachers' readings of and responses to the NCPE. We therefore address what and who have been critical in shaping what the NCPE looks like 'in practice' in state schools in England and Wales and pursue the much talked of gap between policy and practice in education. While retaining this focus on the NCPE in England and Wales, we stress that the conditions and experiences that we identify are far from unique to physical education or indeed these two countries. Rather, they reflect increasingly common pressures and demands in schools that relate to political and economic issues arising world-wide (see for example Apple 1993; Sullivan 1997).

Delivering the National Curriculum: a legal obligation

All state schools in England and Wales were required by law to 'deliver' the NCPE. The ERA established this experience of the curriculum as the legal entitlement of all pupils. However, as we highlighted in Chapter 4, as the development of the NCPE progressed it became apparent that this entitlement would be different in different schools. The changes made to the requirements for the NCPE increasingly called into question the very notion of a 'national' (if that was to mean common) curriculum. Here we pursue how the inherent flexibility in the NCPE texts (the 'scope for slippage', see Chapter 2) was expressed and explored in practice. We discuss the different curricula that came to constitute the NCPE in schools in England and Wales, drawing in particular on data provided by head-teachers and heads of physical education departments from schools throughout one LEA at the time of the development of the NCPE and introduction of LMS (see Appendix A). As well as noting differences within these data, we also point to important similarities and stabilities in responses to the NCPE texts, and highlight what we regard as important limitations to teachers' freedom in implementation. We identify teachers as operating within discursive, economic and ideological frames established by others and/or arising from factors beyond their immediate control and emphasise once again the complex relationships between policy 'content' and the contexts of policy and curriculum development (see Chapter 2).

The practicalities of provision

Much of the emphasis on 'flexibility' in the NCPE related to concerns about the resource implications of the requirements, and the need, therefore, for requirements that could be accommodated within existing (and notably different) levels of resourcing of physical education in schools. Four aspects of resourcing have a critical role in shaping and framing curriculum development and practice in physical education; time; staffing; facilities and funding. Furthermore, there are important interrelationships between these factors that need to be acknowledged if we are to unravel what underpins particular emphases in curricula and the dominance of particular teaching methods. Our research has indicated that it is not sufficient to look merely at the *levels* of resourcing. Rather there are qualitative as well as quantitative dimensions that facilitate and/or inhibit developments, and a number of factors that underpin the resourcing of curriculum development need to be explored.

Physical education: in the second division

In the United Kingdom, as elsewhere, physical education is a subject often regarded as of less value than other 'more academic' subjects, invoking a hierarchy that itself reaches out to a wider culture in academia and industry, that historically has artificially separated thought from action and concomitantly privileged intellectual labour over 'practical' and vocational endeavour. In this culture physical education has struggled to gain recognition as a subject having cognitive and 'academic' dimensions. The structure and arrangements for the National Curriculum reinforced the low status of the subject, and privileged a purportedly non-cognitive performance focus within physical education (see Chapters 3 and 4). The development of the NCPE thus seemed to do little to help strengthen the position or status of the subject in schools. This had particularly significance for the implementation of the NCPE, as the allocation of resources to facilitate and support curriculum development (including timetable time, staff, facilities and funding for provision), was a matter of *competition between school subjects*. This has always been the case in schools. However, the nature of the competition changed significantly with the introduction of 'market conditions and rules' in which self-managing schools had responsibility for limited and at times clearly inadequate resources. Below we illustrate the impact of these conditions upon schools and curriculum development within them.

Running out of time

The allocation of time was one of the most contentious aspects of the development and implementation of the National Curriculum. In the absence of statutory allocations to each subject, time became a hotly contested and increasingly scarce commodity in schools (see Dearing 1993; Graham with Tytler 1993). Concerns about teachers' ability to fulfil the requirements of the NCPE within the time that 'in reality' would be allocated to physical education were directly reflected in the extent of the prescriptive requirements and the number of areas of activity that it was specified that schools would be required to incorporate within their programmes (see Chapters 3 and 4).

The basic allocation of time to physical education would obviously be likely to have a bearing upon the range of activities that could be incorporated in school curricula and/or the depth to which activities could be pursued. 'More time' could result in a better range of experiences being offered and/or be a basis for achieving greater depth of knowledge, understanding and ability in particular activities. However, there were also other important considerations in relation to the timetabling of physical education and the opportunities consequently provided for pupils. In particular the *length* of periods impacted upon the activities that it was feasible for schools to offer. This was a key factor in either facilitating or inhibiting the inclusion in the NCPE of activities requiring the use of off-site facilities. Similarly, the *arrangement* of the periods allocated to physical education shaped the possibilities arising in provision. Whether physical education was timetabled in single or double periods, immediately preceding or following a significant break in the school day, or at the beginning or end of the day, could all affect decisions about what could be included in the NCPE (Penney 1994). For example, one head of physical education explained that the placing of two physical education lessons 'back to back', creating a longer lesson, meant that the department may introduce swimming into the curriculum.

As more of the National Curriculum subjects were introduced, the pressure on school timetables became increasingly apparent. Both headteachers and heads of physical education talked of timetables being 'squeezed' and in some cases, the low status and late arrival of physical education in the National Curriculum meant that physical education was the subject to feel the consequences of this pressure. One head of physical education explained that 'Justification of the subject' was 'more and more crucial' if the department was 'to have a chance of retaining PE time allocation compared to other subjects i.e. science, maths, English' (cited in Penney 1994: 231). The difficulty that schools faced in trying to meet the increasing and competing demands for time as more subjects came 'on line' in the National Curriculum also led to some schools restructuring their school day, changing the length of teaching periods and/or the length of breaks. Any reductions in the length of teaching periods or breaks were a particular concern for physical education teachers. Suggestions such as the shortening of a lunch break were seen as likely to reduce extra-curricular provision and take away important time for changing and travel to off-site facilities. Time is always 'tight' in physical education and these were ongoing concerns for teachers anxious to maximise students' learning.

In addition, and despite the stated entitlement of *all* pupils to the NCPE, some schools continued their established practice of timetabling physical education 'against' a second language. Under these arrangements those pupils choosing to study a second language 'lost' some (often half) of their physical education lessons. Such arrangements not only clearly contradicted schools' legal obligations regarding the delivery of the NCPE, but also demonstrated that guidance from Local Education Authorities (LEAs) (see Chapter 5) was merely that; guidance, that schools could choose to adopt or reject as they saw fit.

After the ERA many teachers also had increasing doubts as to whether amid an array of new demands, they had sufficient **time to teach**. The ERA precipitated a vast increase in administrative work for schools and teachers within them. Teachers of all subjects faced a proliferation of paperwork and meetings associated with the introduction of LMS and the National Curriculum. One head of PE explained that there was 'More paperwork – personal profiles, national curriculum, LMS, Budgeting, development plans etc.' (cited in Penney 1994: 234). Others made very apparent the negative impact of these demands, saying that there had been 'a proliferation of "chat shows" at which little is decided and paperwork which achieves very little', or reflecting that:

All the changes taking place in education have put a far greater workload on staff so much so that it would be quite possible to occupy all your time and not teach! What is desperately needed is a period of stability when teachers can get on with the job they are employed to do – just *teach*

(Ibid.)

Instead, teachers were reporting 'more meetings', 'much more paper-work' and 'more admin' (see Penney 1994). It was also notable that in the light of the introduction of the National Curriculum in 'earlier' subjects and the perceived workload of the assessment requirements for the National Curriculum, the NCPE was expected to 'arrive' with considerable administrative demands. In Seashire (see Chapter 5) these fears were not allayed by the LEA's physical education inspectors. Instead, they were reinforced by the LEA's focus upon the changes in curriculum documentation that should accompany physical education teachers' introduction of the NCPE. For some heads of physical education additional workload was *the* perceived impact of the NCPE on their provision of physical education and sport. Rather than being a focus for curriculum development, the NCPE represented an unwelcome administrative burden (see p. 107). As we indicated in Chapter 4, the administrative demands arising from the National Curriculum were a driving force behind its revision in 1994, when the need for a period of 'stability' was also emphasised and there was a promise of no further changes to requirements for 5 years (see Chapter 4 and Dearing 1993).

Selling the subject . . . and sport

In addition to these pressures of time and administrative workloads, teachers also faced other demands. Schools were now in the business of selling their services to prospective clients. Teachers were therefore expected to contribute to 'marketing activities' and play whatever part they could in promoting a positive public image for their school. Ironically in the light of its invariable low status as a subject, physical education was now seen as having particular marketing potential in some schools. For example, one head of PE explained that 'Staff are more aware of the need for an attractive physical education programme' and others spoke encouragingly of the recognition that physical education and sport could be 'a selling point' for their school (Penney 1994). However, exactly *what* was recognised as physical education's selling point is an important issue to consider, and not all heads of physical education agreed with the emphasis that was being encouraged by senior management and school governors. One head of physical education faced a situation of 'Having to sell our "subject and school" to "win" more pupils' with the result that, in her view, there was an 'over emphasis on "window dressing" instead of getting on with teaching pupils' (cited in Penney 1994: 233). In another school the head of physical education was being 'Pressurised by the head to provide more extra-curricular activities in order to attract more pupils for financial reasons' (ibid.). Others reported 'Extra pressure on *team success*/drop in roll of our school' and '"Encouragement" to produce "winning" teams' (ibid.). These pressures clearly illustrate the influence of the wider contexts of the development of the NCPE, in which specific discourses, noticeably those of sport and of elite performance, were promoted by the public and media, and therefore, it was assumed, desired by the majority of parents that schools were seeking to attract. In these circumstances schools were unlikely to deviate from the dominant discourses. The costs of such deviation, the loss of clientele, could, quite literally, be too great. As Ball observed 'Resistance in this context threatens the survival of the institution' (1993a: 111).

Staffing physical education

The level of staffing of physical education was also a critical factor in relation to the range of activities that could be incorporated in physical education curricula and in determining the quality of teaching and learning in schools. Having more staff in a physical education department was typically associated with extending the range of expertise within the department, and thereby enabling diversification in the activities incorporated in the curriculum. For example, one head of physical education explained that 'we have just employed a new PE mistress and dance will be put back into the curriculum'. Equally, the loss of a member of physical education staff and the consequent absence of a specific area of interest and expertise could place the continued provision of particular activities in jeopardy. The *specific* expertise of physical education staff was certainly critical in shaping the activities offered in or excluded from curricula, such that heads of physical education frequently explained that the content of the following year's programme would be dependent upon 'staffing/specialisms' or 'staffing changes'. The requirements for the NCPE largely legitimated this practice and the flexibility in the requirements facilitated its continuation. It was still the case that differences in the expertise and interests of physical-education teachers would shape the curriculum provided for pupils, and opportunities and experiences would thus be different in different schools.

However, a number of other issues also need to be addressed in exploring the expertise 'available' in physical education. In the implementation of the NCPE we saw that the utilisation of physical education expertise within a school could be limited by factors beyond the control of physical education departments. In particular, decisions made by *senior management* in relation to the timetabling of staff and students were critical in enabling departments to develop the range of activities that they offered. Equally, however, senior management decisions could prevent physical education departments from exploring this potential. At times physical education was regarded as a lower priority than other subjects and specialist physical education staff were then 'removed' from physical education to meet teaching demands in other 'higher priority' subject areas. *Non-specialist staff* were then used to fill these and other gaps arising in physical education teaching. Our research revealed the disturbing extent to which non-specialist staff were used in physical education, and the clear impact that this could have on the quality of teaching and learning in the subject. One head of physical education explained that 'The amount of curricular time taught by non-specialists has increased. Consequently the standard of teaching is lower, as is the quality of learning' (cited in Penney 1994: 218), while another reported that 'There are only two members of staff in the department. We are frequently timetabled alongside non-specialist teachers ... who are far from satisfactory'. Similarly, another head of physical education said that 'non-specialists do their best but it does make keeping up standards trying at times'. The comment that 'We have non-specialists in the dept. *This "leads" the timetable*' (ibid.: 218–19) drew attention to another important issue to consider in relation to non-specialist staffing; the direction in which such staffing may well 'lead' physical education. The following remarks from another head of physical education provided a valuable insight into this matter; 'We have lost a full-time member of PE in the last 2 years. We are staffed by non-specialists with an interest in games' (ibid.: 219). Invariably, participation and/or interest in a particular sport was deemed a qualification for teaching physical education. In these circumstances, it was far from guaranteed that the distinction between physical education and sport that the NCPE working group had emphasised (see Chapter 3) would be upheld or sustained. Furthermore, given the reliance on non-specialist staff, there was every likelihood that games would continue to dominate many curricula. Although the Conservative government and the media continued to claim that games were 'in decline', the reality was that in the majority of schools a disproportionate amount of time and resources was devoted to games as compared to other activities. The NCPE texts produced by central government openly legitimated and promoted this bias (see also Penney 1994; Penney and Evans 1994; Penney and Harris 1997).

In considering the teaching of games in physical education we also need to acknowledge that historically many schools in England and Wales have adopted a *sex differentiated* pattern of provision and/or staffing of activities. Different activities have been included in the curriculum offered to girls as compared to boys, and these have respectively been taught by female and male physical education teachers. This was another feature of established practice that the central government's texts neither required nor encouraged schools and teachers to change, and that we have seen continuing amid the implementation of the NCPE (see also Chapter 8).

Can we afford appointments?

Investigation of non-specialist staffing also served to illustrate the emerging effects of the changing context of schools and schooling after the ERA.

Under LMS staffing costs were the major budget item within schools. Increasingly, the question arising for many headteachers was whether or not their school could afford salary costs. Avoiding appointments and/or appointing at a lower level represented an important saving for schools. In some circumstances, such 'savings' were a matter of necessity if schools were to remain solvent. Faced with a falling roll and thus a reduced income, one headteacher explained that she had little alternative but to 'lose' a member of staff; 'The school is reducing in size. A male PE specialist cannot be replaced in September. Non-specialist staff will be used, alongside 3 remaining specialists' (cited in Penney 1994: 232). In another school the head of PE reported that they were 'losing a member of staff this year even though our numbers are going up. The class ratio for year 7 will be 1:30. We are not happy!!' (cited in Penney 1994: 233). Financial pressures and constraints were clearly a 'whole school issue' after the ERA. However, it was again apparent that subject status played a part in the strategies proposed to counter these constraints. Again physical education could suffer because of both its historical low status and also its late position in the development of the National Curriculum (see Chapters 1 and 3). In one of the schools in Seashire (see Chapter 5), the head of physical education explained that the department faced a situation in which one physical education specialist was 'being taken to teach in humanities more than PE/games and this [was] taking precedence to PE because of National Curriculum implications' (cited in Penny 1994: 232). With non-specialist input to the subject commonplace, other heads of physical education also highlighted that they had a clear interest in appointments being made in other subject areas. One commented that 'Appointments with a PE background would be useful' (ibid.: 221) and some physical education departments were fortunate in receiving this type of indirect boost to their expertise. One head of physical education explained that a newly appointed maths teacher was also a physical education specialist, but at the same time identified that this teacher's contribution to the physical education curriculum would be necessarily limited and that the main help would be in extra-curricular provision. Nevertheless, with schools looking to minimise their total staff numbers, diversity of expertise and flexibility in teaching seemed to be increasingly regarded as attractive qualities in prospective staff.

Facilities for physical education

The facilities available for physical education were an issue that frequently featured in debates concerning the NCPE requirements, with the Conservative central government emphasising that the statutory requirements needed to be able to accommodate differences between schools in this respect. Our research repeatedly highlighted the many ways in which differences in the range, condition, location and availability of facilities for physical education framed curriculum opportunities provided by schools. Certainly these matters shaped the NCPE 'in practice' just as they had influenced the central government's texts (see Chapters 3 and 4).

With a good range of facilities, schools were in a position to offer a broad range of activities, and improvements to facilities contributed towards the development of greater 'breadth and balance' in physical education curricula. For example, one head of physical education reported an improvement in school facilities with the building of a new dance and fitness centre 'so these activities, movement and HRF [health related fitness], will be given curriculum time instead of certain time on games activities' (cited in Penney 1994: 221). Equally, inadequacies and reductions in the facilities available for physical education could have a detrimental impact upon curricula. Some schools had no on-site playing fields, and/or hard court areas, or a gymnasium. In other cases, on-site facilities were inadequate for the number of pupils, with the quality of physical education suffering as a result. One head of physical education reported that for a school of 750 boys there was only a '1.5 size grass pitch, 1 hard court, 1 small gym, some use of small hall' and 'Therefore [a] restricted PE programme' (ibid.: 222). Obviously a lack of indoor facilities was particularly important when adverse weather prevented outdoor activities.

However, even in schools with a comprehensive range of facilities, this aspect of resourcing could still restrict physical education provision. The poor state of repair of indoor and/or outdoor facilities often impacted upon the programmes developed in schools and, in some schools, the introduction of LMS seemed set to increase these problems. There were, for example, reports of departments 'being encouraged to save money on the frequency and quality of our grounds maintenance' (Head of PE, cited in Penney 1994: 235). However, the effects of the introduction of market principles to education were highly differential, with schools and departments within them experiencing very different financial fortunes. As we see below, not all were losers in the context of LMS.

Nevertheless, concerns about the upkeep of facilities and grounds were all the more important in the light of other pressures arising from the ERA; specifically for increased 'efficiency' in the use of school facilities, and thus the development of more use of facilities outside of school hours. Initiating greater community use of school sport facilities was promoted by central government, some LEAs and sports organisations as a way in which schools could look to generate income. One head of PE explained that in a situation in which 'Money is a lot tighter and less', 'Facilities are looking to be hired out more. Money is now foremost in people's minds!' (ibid.: 237). Another reported that there was 'More use of PE facilities by "outside" agencies to "make money"' (ibid.). Other data indicated that while this additional use of facilities may have short-term financial rewards, it did not come without an accompanying cost. In particular, it could place undue (and in the future, expensive) strain on both facilities and equipment and, since this time, these effects have been noted in other reports concerned with the provision and development of physical education and sport in schools (see for example Mason 1995a, 1995b). Also there was a danger that the promotion of community use could threaten pupils' free access to facilities (see also Chapter 5). In one school in Seashire the introduction of charges was expected to reduce provision as 'School clubs run in evenings will now have to pay for use – and may fold' (Head of PE, cited in Penney 1994: 238).

In considering the facilities available for physical education, timetabling arrangements within schools were also again influential. Access to facilities during curriculum time is not something that physical education departments can take for granted. Other claims to indoor facilities (and in particular, examination and dining requirements) could preclude use for physical education, and in turn necessitate compromises in the physical education curriculum. Space within schools, like time and staff, was a matter of competition between subjects within schools, and availability again either facilitated or inhibited the development of breadth and balance in the physical education curriculum.

Notably, the use of local community off-site facilities could increase the range of activities within the physical education curriculum and enable many pupils to experience activities that could not otherwise be provided. Squash courts, swimming pools and golf courses were just some examples of facilities used by schools. Much of the provision of outdoor education activities, particularly residential courses for students, was also reliant upon access to off-site facilities. In Seashire it was significant that the LEA altered its own financial arrangements to enable continued support for these experiences under conditions of LMS (see Penney 1994). Irrespective of such support, however, we saw that use of off-site facilities was not an option for all schools. Some schools were in a fortunate position of having facilities within easy reach, but for others the time and money involved in travelling precluded use. Once again, timetabling arrangements were a key issue shaping opportunities in physical education, and pressures arising from the ERA certainly constrained provision. The length and scheduling of periods for physical education was critical in determining whether or not use of off-site facilities was regarded as feasible and worth while, and after the ERA both the time and money required for this use seemed increasingly scarce. There were thus reports from heads of physical education that 'We are not using [community facility name] so much – lack of time available and cost of hiring', (Head of PE, cited in Penney 1994: 225) and similarly 'less use made of sports centre – financial, lack of timetabled time' (ibid.). The result for these schools was an increasing reliance on on-site facilities, with, in turn, an inevitable reduction in the range of activities incorporated in the physical education curriculum (Penney 1994).

Funding physical education: competing in the internal market

The funding of physical education after the ERA highlighted the subtleties of the policy process and, in particular, the way in which economic and cultural changes arising at a 'whole school' level could impact upon developments in particular subject areas. Essentially the market pressures and discourses that underpinned the creation of competition *between* schools were also evident, adopted and adapted *within* schools. Thus, rather than *directly* precipitating cuts in the financial support for physical education, the ERA brought about notable changes in budgetary arrangements at a whole school level via which physical education was in some cases advantaged, but in others clearly disadvantaged. Just as schools could be regarded as winners or losers in the education market, so there were also winners and losers among subject departments within schools. By virtue of their varying fortunes at both a school and departmental level, physical education departments could then be very differently placed to address the implementation of the NCPE. Not surprisingly, attitudes towards implementation varied according to these fortunes and, just as cost considerations framed the development of the NCPE texts, so curriculum design in schools was inevitably and unavoidably influenced by what was affordable within any one school (Penney 1994; Penney and Evans 1996).

Headteachers' explanations of the budget allocations being made under LMS showed that, like the allocations of funds to schools, department budgets were being determined by a formula that related primarily to pupil numbers. For example, in one school department allocations were on the basis of 'Pupil count (pupil periods taught/week)'. In this case the time that pupils spent in a subject was used in calculations. In other cases an age weighting was incorporated, mirroring formula funding (see Chapters 1 and 5). One headteacher explained that departmental allowances were 'pupil period driven, with older pupils weighted' (cited in Penney 1994: 239). It is worth reflecting that different subjects, by virtue of status, vary in their ability to attract pupils in contexts of student options. In these conditions some subjects may then lack the funding that may be critical to curriculum development. Furthermore, subjects are also allocated different amounts of time in schools. In some schools inequalities in the market-driven funding arrangements were even more explicit. For example, another headteacher explained that allocations were 'made according to a pupil-driven formula plus *agreed* "weightings" for subject areas' (ibid.). In another school the criteria for allocations were the 'number of students, age weighting and type of subject'. In this latter case it was explained that 'PE has a middle range subject weighting of 1.4' (ibid.).

Data from both headteachers and heads of physical education departments indicated that in addition to funding allocations on the above formula basis, many departments could also 'bid' for funding to support specific developments and/or needs. Allocation of these moneys was clearly dependent upon the discretion of the headteacher and/or senior management staff in schools, but also the ability of departments to present a strong case for support. One headteacher highlighted that the physical education department had received a 'low allocation in 1990/91' as it 'could not identify its needs in a coherent form, relating it to curriculum development' (cited in Penney 1994: 240). However, not all departments were equally well placed in terms of how their bids would be received. Perceptions of priorities and status were important and so was the position of physical education late in the National Curriculum development process. There were reports of 'Insufficient funds – priority given to subjects already on stream for National Curriculum means less comes to PE' (Head of PE, cited in Penney 1994: 242) and 'Other curriculum areas demanding more money because of National Curriculum implications. PE still waiting for National Curriculum guidelines so can not compete with other subjects who already have theirs' (ibid.).

Costs of transport and off-site facility hire remained particular areas of concern for physical education departments after the ERA and we saw the detrimental impact that inadequacies in funding could have on the physical education curriculum. It was clear that LEAs' specific responses to LMS were important in determining the moneys available to support future provision (see also Chapter 5). In Seashire there were reports of year 7 swimming being 'abandoned' because of the inability to meet the combined costs associated with provision. Other areas of provision were also threatened by declining standards of facility maintenance, and/or repair or replacement of equipment. The ability of some schools to maintain breadth in their PE curricula was then clearly being placed in jeopardy by the ERA's new funding arrangements for education.

In addition, although we certainly acknowledge that departments occupied different financial positions in facing implementation of the NCPE, we also saw a common and underlying inadequacy in the funding for physical education. In many schools in England and Wales 'voluntary contributions' (see Chapter 5) from parents and fund-raising activities continued to be a critical source of funding for some aspects of provision and in particular the use of off-site facilities. The inequalities inherent in this situation remained overlooked. Not all parents are able to make such contributions and the wealth of parent populations varies widely between schools. Ultimately, these differences may well be reflected in the opportunities offered by different schools.

The rich and the poor in the education market

The above discussion has highlighted that pragmatic concerns relating to resourcing were critical in shaping physical education curricula in schools after the ERA. Pressures, inadequacies in resourcing, and tensions within schools prevailed throughout the implementation of the NCPE. It became evident that discursive and ideological frames operating beyond schools had been adopted within them. Competition between subjects for resources to support development of a National Curriculum was now a common feature of life in schools. However, it was also apparent that particular individuals had a key role to play in determining the respective fortunes of different departments in relation to matters of resourcing. The freedom of heads of physical education to develop the NCPE thus needs to be seen as set within pragmatic boundaries determined by headteachers and senior management staff, and as reflecting, to some degree, the conditions within which senior management decisions were set. In addition, because of their position and influence, the ideological views and interests of headteachers and senior management staff were also seen to shape the relative fortunes of particular subjects. Personal agendas and interests came into play in the policy process. In addressing these influences we highlight that there is a need to consider not merely whether or not support was forthcoming for physical education, but also what aspect of the subject support was being directed towards. Invariably *sport*, rather than physical education, was valued by other (non PE) teachers, and a 'school' (senior management and/or governing body) interest in and commitment to *sport* could well benefit physical education departments. For example, one head of PE explained 'We have definitely benefited under LMS. The deputy head in charge of LMS *is a keen sportsman* and has made extra provision possible from other accounts for one-off items needed to be bought' (cited in Penney 1994: 242). Equally, however, an emphasis on sport could give rise to conflict in relation to the direction and emphases expressed in physical education curricula. Neither senior management, other staff or school governing bodies may be as interested in and supportive of heads of department and/or physical education teachers concerned to pursue interests other than elite sport (see also Chapter 8).

In the implementation of the NCPE in schools there was therefore clearly more than one point at which the discourses privileged in the government's texts could be reinforced or challenged, new discourses come into play and slippage occur in implementation. Senior management staff were key figures in the policy process together with heads of departments. In considering the potential for the contestation and adaptation of policy, it is also inappropriate to portray physical education departments as united around particular discourses and values. Within departments there was as much capacity for contrast and conflict as there was for consensus, with individuals having different priorities and interests in their subject. In the section below we consider further how these relative freedoms and influences were expressed in the implementation of the NCPE.

The NCPE – from policy to practice

What then, in market driven and contested conditions, were the key features of teachers' responses to the NCPE texts issued by central and local government? What did the NCPE look like in different schools, with varying levels of human and physical resources and different interests in and ideological orientations to physical education?

A critical point to recall is that in many respects the NCPE had been designed to accommodate long-standing differences between schools, and the differential effects of the ERA. Certainly the NCPE could not be expected to look the same in different schools. It is also important to remember the degree to which the structure and emphasis of the NCPE mirrored established and existing practice in schools. In combination, these characteristics gave rise to a situation in which implementation of the NCPE could mean very limited change in practice in schools. The flexibility, gaps and omissions in the government's texts, and their explicit activity and games focus presented the opportunity for creativity in implementation (see Chapter 8), but equally, for the adoption and adaptation of requirements within essentially unchanged programmes. Given the relative exclusion of teachers from the development process, the rushed nature of development, the absence of professional development opportunities and support in implementation, and the increasingly demanding contexts in which teachers were working, it is perhaps not surprising that the latter response emerged as a common characteristic of the implementation of the NCPE. Rather than the NCPE being a focus for development of physical education curricula, in many instances its requirements and discourses were largely subsumed within those already established and dominant in schools. For example one head of physical education anticipated 'Minor changes. I feel our curriculum is very much in line with kind of ideas coming from Interim Report for PE. Very wide ranging and balanced curriculum' (cited in Penney 1994: 245). Another predicted 'Little change of content but anticipate greater time spent on assessment' (ibid.). In the main the changes anticipated by heads of physical education were confined to a 'surface level'. Several heads of physical education anticipated that they would have to make an addition to the range of activities that they offered in the curriculum, in particular to meet the requirement to include an aesthetic activity at key stage 3. However, those areas of activity that were already included in curricula were invariably regarded as meeting the NCPE requirements and therefore not in need of review or development. One head of PE explained that with the exception of introducing one new area 'we're covering all the areas ... so the implications aren't as great as people think' (ibid.: 260). The anticipation that the introduction of the NCPE would mean a 'Rethink of course content, its delivery and assessment – all time consuming but beneficial' (ibid.: 246) was extremely rare, and the fears that had been expressed by one of the working group (Murdoch 1992) that elements that were now implicit in the NCPE texts could be ignored or overlooked, seemed fully justified.

Thus we saw in schools that 'slippage' in the policy process rarely took the form of contestation of, resistance to or deviation from the Conservative government's interests and priorities. More often than not the established practice displayed the very biases that the government's texts had legitimated and reinforced, and indicated continuity in physical education under the label of the 'reform'. Physical education curricula had always varied between schools and yet at the same time displayed commonality in structure and emphases (notably on the teaching of team games). The introduction of the NCPE did not change this. The central government's text allowed for pragmatic issues and concerns to continue to shape curricula and, after the ERA, school contexts reinforced the importance of pragmatic concerns in curriculum planning. Far from being creatively explored, many of the 'gaps' in the government's texts (such as how 'permeating themes' should be expressed in curriculum design and teaching, or expectations regarding assessment procedures) thus seemed similarly to be omissions in practice (see also Chapter 8 and OFSTED 1995; Office of Her Majesty's Chief Inspector of Schools in Wales (OHMCI) 1995; Clay 1997a, 1997b).

A further factor underpinning the limited changes in practice was the position of physical education late in the National Curriculum development process. One head of physical education explained that 'Observation of other subject areas spending hours being "proactive" only to see their efforts wasted due to changes in the National Curriculum from week to week has led to a reserved and cautious outlook' (cited in Penney 1994: 247). This department and many others were understandably content to wait for the final version of the NCPE before planning their response, rather than to instigate what could prove to be premature and inappropriate changes. The result of this approach, however, was that when the statutory orders were finally issued in 1992 there was inadequate time for comprehensive curriculum review and development before implementation was due to commence.

As well as considering the content and structure of the National Curriculum, we should address other pedagogical concerns. The National Curriculum made few explicit recommendations regarding the **teaching methods** to be employed in its delivery. Although elements of child-centredness remained in the NCPE texts issued by the government, as Bernstein's (1971, 1990) analysis of the curriculum points out, the strongly classified structure provided for the NCPE (celebrating boundaries and distinctions between different areas of activity), seemed likely to generate and sustain distinctly hierarchical relations in classrooms, and a reliance upon didactic teaching methods directed towards the transmission of the skills, competencies and knowledge predetermined by the National Curriculum texts, rather than more innovative, exploratory and pupil-centred methods. In the absence of guidance and encouragement in the NCPE documents for use of varied and particularly pupil-centred pedagogies, and with little if any professional development addressing such matters in implementation (see Chapter 5), we could hardly expect that the NCPE would encourage a review or revision of practices and traditions that historically had become a long-standing feature of physical education teaching in England and Wales. The relative neglect of pedagogical critique remains a characteristic of the implementation of the NCPE (see OFSTED 1995; OHMCI 1995; Clay 1997a, 1997b) and, for us, a matter of concern that we return to in Chapter 8.

Having emphasised this absence of change, we should note, however, the ways in which the introduction of the NCPE did have a clear impact upon physical education departments. As indicated in Chapter 5, the most obvious and immediate demand arising in implementation was for change in the documentation within physical education departments. In the words of one teacher implementation was 'a case of re-writing rather than totally reorganising' (cited in Penney 1994: 260). The other foreseen changes and concerns centred upon the assessment, reporting and recording of students' learning in physical education. These were concerns that the texts issued by central government repeatedly failed to address. They provided no detailed comment and clarification on these matters, but instead indicated that it would be for individual schools to address how they would meet the requirements of the National Curriculum. For teachers working in times of ever increasing calls for accountability and 'evidence of achievement', these were matters of priority and a clear source of anxiety. Neither the LEA inspectors nor the government curriculum agencies seemed willing to respond to teachers' needs and concerns and, once again, we should therefore not be surprised that we face reports that development of assessment, recording and reporting in physical education is lacking in both the secondary and primary sectors (see OFSTED 1995; OHMCI 1995; Clay 1997a, 1997b).

No change in a new ERA

Far from signalling review, reform and standardisation, the implementation of the NCPE reinforced differences in the practices of different schools and confirmed established and familiar practices of curriculum provision and teaching. It was all too clear that pupils across England

and Wales would not enjoy a common experience of a 'broad and balanced' physical education; the rhetorical intentions of the ERA and an NCPE. Many interrelated factors played a part in shaping this outcome and determining what in any one school the NCPE would look like in practice. The flexibility inherent in the NCPE requirements gave the impression of placing schools, departments and teachers in a position of independence, and according them the authority to determine the experiences and opportunities that would constitute the NCPE. However, that autonomy often had to be set in school contexts that featured unfavourable and unsupportive market conditions, and that therefore placed notable limits upon the freedoms of teachers to review or develop the curriculum and teaching of physical education. Thus there was, ironically, often very little difference between the narrow restorationist requirements of government policy, and extant practices in schools. Certainly, in our view, the NCPE could be seen to have failed to prompt the progress (and particularly the encouragement of greater equity in physical education) that a policy development on this scale seemed to hold the potential for. In Chapter 8 we discuss these matters further as we consider the strengths and weaknesses of contemporary physical education in the light of the dominance of particular discourses. We examine the largely unrealised potential in England and Wales and elsewhere for the development of 'alternative' discourses, curricula and pedagogies in physical education that seek to promote greater equity and that are sensitive to the changing socio-cultural conditions of a post modern age. First, however, we return to our task of providing a theoretical framework that can adequately embrace the complexities of policy that we saw emerge in and shape the NCPE in England and Wales.

Summary

All state schools in England and Wales had a legal obligation to implement the National Curriculum for Physical Education. The statutory requirements were such that the NCPE could be expected to look quite different in different schools. Ultimately a complex combination of factors played a part in determining what in any given school pupils would experience as the NCPE. Particularly in the conditions arising from LMS, matters of resourcing were destined to shape the opportunities that would be provided. Time, staffing, facilities and funding for physical education were all influential in this respect, and were also a focus for competition between subjects and departments in schools. The potential for physical education departments and the teachers within them to be innovative in implementation was in important respects conditional upon decisions made by headteachers and senior management staff, and both pragmatic and ideological interests came into play in those decisions. Although physical education may often be seen as a low status subject, 'sport' has a higher status within and beyond schools and some physical education departments felt the benefit of sport being pursued as a 'selling point' for a school. Overall, however, the picture was of departments being differentially placed to meet the demands of the NCPE and of many teachers lacking the incentive and support to be proactive and innovative in implementation. There was a notable tendency for the new requirements to be accommodated within largely unchanged patterns of provision and there was a convenient 'match' between the NCPE texts issued by central government and many long-standing practices in physical education in England and Wales. Thus in important respects, the slippage seen in implementation of the NCPE in individual schools featured consistencies in terms of the interests and discourses privileged in physical education, rather than changes or deviations in these terms. The introduction of the NCPE could therefore be seen as having largely failed to encourage critical reflection upon contemporary practices.

Further reading

The edited collection *Sense and Nonsense and the National Curriculum* (Barber and Graham 1993, Falmer Press) includes chapters that provide further insights into schools' implementation of the National Curriculum in the context of local management of schools. Other work specifically concerned with the implementation National Curriculum for Physical Education has included:

Crutchley, D.H. and Robinson, L. (1996) 'Teachers' Perceptions of "Planning", "Performing" and "Evaluating" within National Curriculum Physical Education', *The Bulletin of Physical Education* 32(1): 46–54.
Curtner-Smith, M.D., Kerr, I.G. and Hencken, C.L. (1995) 'The Impact of the National Curriculum Physical Education on Teachers' Behaviours Related with Pupils' Skill Learning: A Case Study in One English Town', *British Journal of Physical Education Research Supplement* 16(Summer): 2–12.

Shaughnessy and Price (1995) have specifically addressed implementation of the NCPE in primary schools. See for example:

Shaughnessy, J. and Price, L. (1995) 'Physical Education in Primary Schools. A Whole New Ball Game', *The Bulletin of Physical Education,* 31(1): 14–20.
Shaughnessy, J. and Price, L. (1995) 'Physical Education in Primary Schools. What's been going on since September 1992?', *The Bulletin of Physical Education* 31(2): 34–42.

Reports of inspection findings since the implementation of the NCPE are also available. See for example:

Clay, G. (1997) 'Standards in Primary Physical Education: OFSTED 1995–6', *Primary PE Focus* (Autumn): 4–6.

Clay, G. (1997) 'Standards in Primary and Secondary Physical Education: OFSTED 1995–96', *British Journal of Physical Education* 28(2): 5–9.

Office for Standards in Education (OFSTED) (1995) *Physical Education. A Review of Inspection Findings 1993/4.* London: HMSO

Office of Her Majesty's Chief Inspector of Schools in Wales (OHMCI) (1995) *Report by HM Inspectors. Survey of Physical Education in Key Stages 1, 2 and 3.* Cardiff: OHMCI.

Chapter 7

Power in the policy game

It isn't easy studying policy and perhaps particularly education policy, which, as we have seen, is imbued with competing interests and political intent. Certainly we have often felt that we have been working on shifting socio-cultural sands (difficult enough in itself), but also in and through discursive dust storms that were politically driven, and intended to dictate the direction of travel and obscure the nature and boundaries of the educational terrain. The preceding chapters have highlighted these characteristics of the policy process in education and its many complexities; for example, the dynamic interactions between different (and often in appearance, unrelated) policies, and the involvement of many sites and individuals in determining how policies issued by central government are reflected in the practices of LEAs and schools. We have presented data that illustrate both strengths and critical shortcomings in our own and others' theorising of this process and that have reinforced the need for concepts that can grasp its many dimensions and in particular, the *inequalities in power relations* that are inherent in the process. Despite our commitment to deconstruct the divide between policy 'makers' and 'implementors' and to emphasise the creative potential in implementation, we have seen the very different status of various individuals in the policy process, and most obviously, the limited influence of teachers in shaping a curriculum that they were charged to deliver. We have emphasised that many of the decisions made at the early stages of the policy process retained a critical influence *throughout* the process and thus draw attention to the corresponding limits to discursive freedoms.

We have presented the concept of **frame** as a tool to describe the progressive and at the same time constrictive aspects of the process. In our view this concept helps us to locate and critique the slippage that we have witnessed 'between' various policy texts and, in particular, draw attention to the limits as well as the possibilities for individuals to pursue new discourses and new directions when responding to and implementing policies. The concept of frame has thus been central to our attempts to understand the inequalities inherent in the policy process in relation to 'who has what say' with regard to policy and the *particular* interests and discourses that came to be privileged, or equally subordinated or excluded, from the policies and practices of physical education. Using this concept we have sought to develop a theory capable of pursuing 'how existing curricula originates, is reproduced, metamorphoses and responds to new prescriptions ... of how people involved in the ongoing production and reproduction of curriculum act, react and interact' (Goodson 1991: 167). Usefully, a conceptualisation centring on the notion of frames can embrace the concept of discourse that has been so central to our own and others' critiques of recent policy developments in England and Wales, but, at the same time, can also draw attention to the need to accompany this focus with a concern for other key factors in the policy process and, in particular, structural issues. In the preceding chapters we have illustrated that the visibility of discourses is an expression of power relations and inequalities in the policy process. In searching for the sources of these inequalities our data have pointed to the critical influence of the 'arrangements for policy' (Hill 1980). As the ex-chair of the National Curriculum Council has emphasised, the development of the National Curriculum in England and Wales was quite clearly in these respects, 'a lesson for us all' (Graham with Tytler 1993). Our research has left us inclined to echo the view of other policy researchers, that it is in the control of these arrangements for policy formulation that 'decisive' and determining power ultimately lies. In Clegg's words, the central feature of power lies in the 'fixing of the terrain for its own expression' (1989: 183). This is in line with Lukes' (1974) identification of the 'third dimension of power', 'involving the exercise of power to shape people's preferences, so that neither overt nor covert conflicts exist' (Ham and Hill 1984: 67). Apple has similarly emphasised that the 'success' of the Reagan administration in the USA, and of the Thatcher and Major governments in Britain 'should not only be evaluated in electoral terms. They also need to be judged by their success in disorganising other more progressive groups, in *shifting the terms of political, economic and cultural debate on to the terrain favoured by capital and the Right*' (1993: 21, our emphasis). Thus Apple (1993) points to the significance of the fact that 'The Right in the United States and Britain has thoroughly renovated and reformed itself' (ibid.) and in this process has *moved debate on education on to their own terrain* 'of "tradition", standardization, productivity, and industrial needs' (ibid.: 23). Like Apple, our interest has been in showing how such shifts have been achieved. Recently Taylor *et al.* (1997) reinforced the importance in this respect of bureaucratic arrangements for policy, stressing the need to deconstruct the divide between policy formulation and *administration*, and to see both politicians and bureaucrats as being involved in both activities. Our data and that of Graham (1996; see also Graham with Tytler 1993) certainly bear testimony to this observation, and point to the significance of arrangements that not only shape the ground upon which policy is laid but that also set the rules by which the 'policy game' is played. In the development of the NCPE, policy rules were undoubtedly critical in determining the form that the NCPE ultimately took as both policy and practice.

Throughout our exploration of the different sites involved in the making and implementation of the NCPE, we have also seen that structural, economic, political, ideological and discursive frames provide a critical sense of location (in time and space) for the policy process and for the 'creation' of frames within it. The significance in policy developments of 'discourses surrounding discourses' (Apple 1982) has been very apparent and we have seen the ways in which 'old', extant and well established frames become embedded in and influence 'new' frames. It has been evident that frames may have origins in contexts that are not always immediately apparent or easy to identify, but that we need to uncover if we are to understand how, when, and why they arise and, critically, whose interests they serve.

The relationship between different frames in the policy process is undoubtedly complex. In particular we may be inclined to think that economic, political and ideological frames *determine* the discursive frames that arise in the policy process. However, the ability of an individual, site or agency to adopt a particular political or ideological standpoint, or pursue a specific economic agenda, is itself dependent on discursive resources, and is therefore subject to the operation of discursive frames. Equally, the origins of structures can be debated. Ranson (1986) explains that:

> The state is a structuring of power and values. The organization of government, law and finance embody society's dominant beliefs about the distribution of power and control and about whether power should be concentrated or diffused. Yet those beliefs about the organizing of power themselves reflect values about the form that economic and social relations might take in civil society.
>
> (Ranson 1986: 205)

In Lundgren's view 'The structural conditions created by ongoing economic and social development constitute the outer constraints for changes in education, as well as determining its structure' (1977: 10).

What constitutes structure is itself problematic. Indeed, both the meaning of the term and the nature of structural forms have occupied the attention of social scientists for many years (Giddens 1979). The perspective adopted may be national or global, micro, macro, or meso. Although theoretical models may capture a global view of social systems and structures, inevitably empirical research and analysis can represent only part of 'the picture' and in this case only a 'piece of the action' in the policy process. Our own research can be seen to have fallen short in the degree to which it has located the national within global developments, but it has perhaps served to emphasise the importance of national and local mediations of global influences (see also Dale and Robertson 1997). Ball (1997) has remained critical, however, of the relative inability of much policy research in the UK to address global dimensions.

The concept of 'structure' also implies a phenomenon that is always and inevitably more than the sum of its parts, and embedded in which are social rules and power relations that are carried or relayed within social relations and actions, including the policy process. Structures addressed in our analysis cannot and should not, therefore, be reified; regarded as fixed or unchangeable objects. While addressing notions of structure we have seen the dangers in policy analyses of both disproportionately undermining, or, in contrast, over-emphasising, either human agency, the freedom of individuals to shape developments, or the 'control' and 'constraint' inherent in the process. Dale, warning of the dangers of overly focusing on 'process', has argued that some researchers of education policy have tended:

> ... to stress processes rather than structures, ideologies rather than institutions, and the composition of competition between different interested parties rather than the rules of the competition or the terrain on which it took place.
>
> (1992: 21)

Meanwhile Lingard has seen a dichotomy between 'state control' and 'policy cycle' models in relation to these matters, and has taken the view that:

> ... the former tends to over emphasise the power of the state in policy implementation and fails to consider the impact of internal state structures on policy formulation, while the latter amplifies the power of schools and teachers to modify such policies and across time has neglected state structures.
>
> (1993: 1)

Stephen Ball's work has been particularly criticised for failing to fully address structural issues (see Henry 1993). The basis for this criticism (perhaps to a great extent unjustified) is Ball's privileging of a Foucauldian view of power which emphasises dispersal, rather than control and/or possession (Ball 1990b). In this view power is exercised, or practised, rather than possessed and so circulates through every related force, and requires us to examine the way in which power, as a recursive force and form of practice, is embedded and embodied in every aspect, agent and agency involved in the policy process (Evans, Davies and Penney 1994). However, while critiques of Ball's work prompt caution when examining the productive and constructive dimensions of power, they also perhaps understate those elements of Foucault's thesis which point to the more enduring, less 'negotiable' features of power and constraint. Smart (1983) for example, reminds us that Foucault does not deny structure. Rather, he denies that power relations are derived from institutions and instead urges attention to be directed towards the mechanisms and preconditions of power, and in particular the conditions upon which the effectiveness of these mechanisms depends.

Our own view, which resonates with that of Ranson, is that the type of theory needed in addressing policy has to be 'rooted in the agency of actors indicating the way social arrangements are continually produced and reproduced', yet also 'aware of the deep seated constraints of the "system requirements"' (1985: 119). Raab also stresses that 'human agency must be taken seriously in explanations of policy. But so, too, must the context of action within structures and processes located at other sites, or enveloping all of them, and providing the constraints or opportunities for action' (1994: 25).

Power in relation to policy

Our interests in exploring power in relation to policy can be linked to a number of questions: who is involved and has what say in the construction of education policy?; what values are being pursued and in whose interests?; what underpins the dominance of particular voices and discourses?; what constitutes power in these terms? Is it the ability to 'be heard', to bring particular discourses into play and to achieve their acceptance, legitimation and reinforcement?

At one level our identification of different types of frame enables us to pursue the distribution of power and, specifically, the scope for different sites and individuals to define policy content and the mechanisms of its 'production'. At another, it prompts us to pursue the nature of power itself in relation to policy. In each of the sites explored we have seen that power was not only about discourse but also about one's position and status in the policy process (see also Ball 1993b). Our analysis identified different dimensions to power; discursive, structural, economic, and also indicated that power is 'not a commodity or an object', but, rather, is *relational*. It is about a balance between freedom and constraint, **agency and structure**. These latter matters are critical in determining the relations inherent in the policy process, the dispersal of power, and the obvious inequalities in that dispersal. At all of the sites we have seen that 'there is agency and there is constraint in relation to policy – this is not a sum-zero game' (Ball 1993b: 13), but we have also noted that the balances between control and agency that different players enjoy are far from equal. In Ball's view, policy analysis 'requires not an understanding that is based on constraint or agency but on the changing relationships between constraint and agency' (1993b: 13–14). In our view any consideration of this relationship demands that structural issues and arrangements established for policy development are addressed.

Many of the models and conceptualisations of policy presented to date fail, in our view, to adequately capture the dynamic nature of the relationships between possibilities and constraints in relation to policy. We do not pretend to have a solution to this problem and indeed can see flaws inherent in the model and concepts that we propose. However, critical reflection upon both our own and others' modest theoretical insights may help us to clarify not only the questions worth asking in education policy research, but also the means of addressing them, and thereby furthering an understanding of a complex phenomenon.

Bowe *et al.* (1992) have moved us some way towards such an understanding. They have described the policy process in relation to three policy contexts: (i) the 'context of influence . . . where public policy is normally initiated. It is here that policy discourses are constructed'; (ii) the 'context of policy text production' concerned with representations of policy, which may involve formal and informal texts or speeches; and (iii) the 'context of practice', in which responses to the texts are experienced (Bowe *et al.* 1992: 19). Furthermore they identify that 'struggle' is a feature of all three contexts and is inherent in the construction of a policy *and* the production and interpretation of texts, and stress that a response to a text inevitably involves interpretation and re-creation. Bowe *et al.* thus draw attention to the capacity for policies to be contested and adapted *throughout* the course of their production and implementation. However, their labelling of contexts can be seen to be problematic and to imply the existence of distinct domains of social practice and stages in the policy process, each of which is essentially associated with a different 'level' of extant social structure. For example, they describe the context of influence in relation to the role of government, committees and national bodies in the process, and, in outlining the context of policy text production, focus attention on the role of more formal 'bodies' such as the NCC and DES. Finally they explain the context of practice in relation to practice in schools. Underlying Bowe *et al.*'s analysis is the remaining and problematic conceptual distinction between policy makers and practitioners, and between text production and practice. Consequently their explanations appear to omit or subsume the 'overlap' in the roles of different individuals and policy sites, and to overlook that at *all* sites we can see aspects of the creation of policy and discourses; texts are produced and 'practices' arise.

Bernstein's penetrating analysis of the production of pedagogic discourse also identifies three contexts, with an implicit hierarchy. These he terms the 'primary context', in which the development of texts occurs via a process of 'primary contextualization' in which 'new ideas are selectively created, modified, and changed and where specialized discourses are developed, modified, or changed' (1990: 59); a 'secondary context', involving the 'selective reproduction' of educational discourse in schools and a 'recontextualizing context', in which 'positions, agents, and practices' function 'to regulate the circulation of texts between the primary and secondary contexts' (ibid.: 60). Implicit once again is a distinction between 'making' and 'implementation' and the association of these phenomena with a structural hierarchy. The state is identified as a focus for activities within the primary context, LEAs are identified as possible recontextualising agents, and reproduction is said to occur in schools. Although Bernstein reminds us that in the process of recontextualisation a text is transformed such that 'the text is no longer the same text' (ibid.), his stress on the *re*production of texts effectively subordinates at least some of the capacity for 'making' or 'production' to occur after a text has left the primary context, and seems to restrict analysis of, for example, the scope for LEAs and schools to actively engage in the processes of 'making' and 'production'. Nevertheless Bernstein presses us to acknowledge variations in the influence of different sites in different contexts, and to explore the distribution of power within the system and specifically the role of the state in determining relations and movements within and between the various contexts. The detail and sophistication of Bernstein's work cannot be detailed here (see Sadovnik 1995; Atkinson, Davies and Delamont 1995). Suffice to say that Bernstein has provided us with powerful concepts to employ in policy analyses, that can help us better understand both the connections between processes at different levels and sites and to also see the potential spaces to be explored within them (see also Penney 1998a).

Bernstein's work is particularly helpful when addressing the relations between policy and the organisation and content of pedagogical practice. As mentioned in Chapter 3, in Bernstein's terms 'classification' refers to 'relations between categories, whether these categories are between agencies, between discourses, between practices' (1996: 20). He stresses that power always operates on and is expressed through these relations and 'in this way, power establishes legitimate relations of order' (1996: 19). So, for example, the strongly classified curriculum of physical education may have an important bearing not only on how the subject matter of physical education stands in terms of value and status in relation to other subject areas, but also how then within the subject those areas of the curriculum, for example, stereotypically defined as 'men's physical cultures', are positioned in relation to women's; or local/community cultures positioned in relation to school curriculum cultures; 'able' in relation to 'less able', and so on. For Bernstein the boundaries and boundary maintenance are the key to maintaining and strengthening or, equally, challenging, the principle of classification.

Control, in Bernstein's view, is about the limits set to what is thinkable, unthinkable, and to what constitutes legitimate communication in the pedagogical process and thus, in turn, what is recognised as legitimate and valued knowledge. From this point of view, control is always articulated by and expressed through 'frames'. Frames 'legitimate forms of communication appropriate to the different categories', socialise individuals into these relationships and, critically, carry 'the boundary relations of power' (Bernstein 1996: 19; see below). In regulating relations within pedagogical contexts frames generate and legitimate particular forms of communication (the nature of talk and the kinds of spaces constructed), in effect determining whose and what voices and actions can be recognised, meet with approval and be heard. Thus the classification and framing carried by and constructed through the curriculum of physical education (i.e. the NCPE) are likely to have a powerful impact at one level upon the developing identities of children and young people, determining not only what they learn to value as physical culture, but also how they, *vis-à-vis* their culture, class, sex or ability, are positioned in relation to it, and to the subject matter of physical education. Children learn what elements of and whose physical cultures are valued in the curriculum. Frames thus determine whose skills and abilities are recognised, heard and valued in physical education, and how children learn to think about and value their own and others' physicality, as well as their own and others' relationships to the physical cultures that feature in schools and the wider communities. Perhaps the important point to stress here, however, is that while Bernstein's use of the term frame presses us to pay attention to the ways in which pedagogical contexts shape children's identities and consciousness, our analysis has also shown how important it is to acknowledge that teachers are both framed by the discursive structures, requirements and resources of the curriculum and its delivery, and are themselves framing the learning opportunities made available to children. Teachers (males, female, those variously interested in dance or gymnastics, or games teaching, or swimming) as well as children have been differently framed and positioned, according to their experiences, aspirations and expertise, in relation to the requirements of the National Curriculum for Physical Education. Thus we can ask what skills and which teachers have been elevated or disenfranchised and alienated by the requirements of the NCPE? (See also Chapter 8.)

Policy, change and research in education

In one way or another all of the above mentioned researchers of policies and practices in education, remind us that the relationship between policy and change 'is an ambiguous one, given that change certainly occurs regardless of policy interventions, and that policy can result (intentionally or otherwise) in little or no change' (Taylor *et al.* 1997: 153). Furthermore, it is vitally important to consider curriculum changes in relation to changes occurring within the wider society and global contexts of which they are part and with which they interact. In this respect much of what we have attempted to achieve in this text bears witness to Whitty's (1997) claim that sociology has an important contribution to make not just to an understanding of contemporary education policy but also to the future development of education policy and practice in schools. Significant socio-cultural and economic changes are now taking place in many parts of the world. As Whitty points out, these have been reflected in the UK in endeavours to restructure and de-regulate state education policy, disband centralised educational bureaucracies and create in their place devolved systems of schooling, entailing significant degrees of autonomy and a variety of forms of schools-based management and administration. These changes which 'have been linked to an increased emphasis on parental choice and on competition between diversified and specialised forms of provision, thereby creating what we now call "quasi markets" in educational services' (Whitty 1997: 122) and are, as we have seen, expressed in and frame the practices of physical education. Furthermore, they constrain the possibilities for innovation and change in physical education in the direction of greater equity. Our data leave us as sceptical as Whitty about the more extravagant claims of those who espouse Conservative and post modern ideals. As he points out, part of the appeal of recent reforms to Conservatives and (some) advocates of the 'post modern' has rested in their declared intention to encourage diversity in education and the growth of different types of school responsive to the need of particular communities and groups. However, our data lend considerable weight to Whitty's view that once the claimed benefits are grounded empirically in the lives of teachers and pupils in schools they soon begin to sound hollow. Much of what we have reported suggests that the 'new arrangements' for education, and physical education within it, 'seem to be just a more sophisticated and intensified way of reproducing traditional distinctions between different types of school and between the people who attend them' (Whitty 1997: 124). Our data endorse research findings which have found that for those schools ill placed to capitalise on their market position, 'the devolution of responsibility can merely lead to the devolution of blame' (ibid.: 127).

Much of our preceding analysis has emphasised the severe *limits* to the changes that teachers are able to make to the curriculum, and in particular the constraining and demanding contexts of contemporary schooling. Teachers' relative exclusion from the development of the NCPE further exacerbated this problem; quashing their sense of professionalism and dampening any residual enthusiasm for innovative implementation. Ball has stressed that:

> Policies do not normally tell you what to do; they create circumstances in which the range of options available in deciding what to do are narrowed or changed. A response must still be put together, constructed in context, off-set against other expectations.
>
> (1993b: 12)

And more recently has again emphasised the creativity that is inherent and necessary in responses (Ball 1997). Repeatedly we have seen that the ERA incorporated and precipitated many expectations and created particular conditions in schools. Together these served to reduce the options available for innovative activity in implementation of the National Curriculum. Thus while not denying the diversity of those conditions, neither can we ignore the overarching frames. As Gerwitz *et al.* have acknowledged 'Clearly, the framework of national policy is crucial and this impacts upon all schools to some degree. There is no escape from the effects of the market system' (1995: 87). Wallace has similarly observed that 'The combination of policy instruments may not have secured universal implementation in line with ministers' expectations, but it does appear to have delimited the range of local responses' (1998: 212–13).

However, despite the limits and constraints inherent in both the texts and the contexts that we have explored, there remain possibilities for the expression of alternative interests and values in physical education. Like Gerwitz *et al.* (1995) we thus also stress that the multi-level interpretation and mediation of policy remains critical. Discourses, even those privileged and carrying the weight of government legislation, cannot be all consuming or completely regulate teacher action. As Maw points out:

> A too ready acceptance of Foucault's proposition that we do not speak discourse, the discourse speaks us, masks the fact that actors employ discourses with varying degrees of naivety, reflectiveness and purpose, and change them in the process.
>
> (1993: 57)

The indication here is that even within very restrictive discursive frames, there is the potential for adaptation, resistance and deviation, for the expression of an 'alternative voice' (Bernstein 1996). There are it seems critical limits in the degree to which interpretations of policy can be directed, 'controlled' and constrained either by the state or any other powerful significant others in the policy process. In Wallace's words 'nobody has a monopoly on power' (1998: 199) and opportunities remain for the development of 'counter-policies' (ibid.). For example, we have seen that while the NCPE working group had no choice but to adopt the Secretary of State's restorationist discourse, they did so with a specific purpose in mind. They attempted to embed an educational discourse, privileging the child as the focus of physical education and the inseparability of cognitive and practical endeavour, within the government's discursive frame (see Chapter 3). Although the subsequent stages of the development of the NCPE showed that the working group themselves had a *limited* capacity to influence the policy process, their actions none the less ensured that at least some seed-bed opportunities for innovation remained in the text that teachers could potentially exploit and explore. Not all would take this opportunity of course. Physical education teachers and teacher educators will vary in both their reflectiveness and the purpose with which they employ the various discourses of the NCPE. We are thus reminded that there are always multiple readings of any text, and that meanings too are multiple and may be contradictory (Apple 1993). Encouragingly, to acknowledge this is to reposition teachers centrally in debates about what ultimately physical education 'looks like', the values that it promotes, the children that it engages with and offers opportunities to. We do not deny that any consideration of power 'requires consideration of imperfect exchanges under imperfect market conditions' (Clegg 1989: 216) and that the imperfections are constraining, but we also see a need to centre analysis not on these constraints; but rather on the possibilities for positive action that remain within them. When texts are de- and then re-located, power relations change, such that 'In the new context, the knowledge *re*producers have more power, and the knowledge is integrated around a different set of political and cultural needs and principles' (Apple 1993: 68) and in this process is transformed. In effect the *transformation* and *reproduction* of knowledge occur simultaneously. The hard task for the policy analyst is to identify the relational elements of continuity and change.

This again draws attention to the fundamental tensions in our analysis, between identifying opportunities or 'spaces' for innovation, but then indicating that the direction and scope of change may well be strongly framed. Clearly individuals may construct their own interpretations and responses to policy, but without always either questioning or being aware of what and who informs and has framed those constructions. Apple's attempt to conceptualise this relational balance of power is helpful. He emphasises that 'the powerful are not *that* powerful. The politics of official knowledge are the politics of accords or compromises' (1993: 10) but at the same time reminds us that compromises are, of course, 'not compromises between or among equals. Those in dominance almost always have more power to define what counts as a need or a problem and what an appropriate response to it should be' (ibid.). Although this smacks of attempting to eat and keep your conceptual cake, the position does help us avoid leaving the reader feeling powerless. Apple (1993) goes on to stress that 'these compromises are never stable. They almost always leave or create space for more democratic action' (ibid.).

In the next chapter we therefore explore these possibilities empirically. We centre attention on issues of what, after the ERA and the National Curriculum for Physical Education, teachers can and cannot do in terms of curriculum innovation and change, and hope to demonstrate that the relationship between curriculum and curriculum theory need not and should not be one of 'profound alienation' (Goodson 1991). In looking for further possibilities for change within the context and constraints of the NCPE we are also recognising another limitation of our own research. Ball has emphasised that there are inherent problems in attempting to draw conclusions from 'time-limited' or 'snapshot' studies about changes that 'take place slowly, almost imperceptibly over time' (1997: 267). Like Ball we would agree that we need to question at what point we can justifiably draw conclusions about the effects of policy, and, in the case of the NCPE, acknowledge and emphasise that its effects are certainly ongoing.

Summary

The complexities of policy development and implementation are as difficult to describe as they are to adequately explain. They are processes that are not either easily accommodated within or accounted for by the theoretical frameworks and concepts that have conventionally been brought to bear on education policy in the United Kingdom and elsewhere. Recent developments in social theory potentially advance our understandings of these processes, and in particular the range of different influences that play upon policy and curricula, and the ongoing and shifting balance between 'freedom' or 'licence' and 'constraint' in policy developments inside and outside schools. This balance is both of central interest and an ongoing dilemma for policy analysts who routinely need to address the structural dimensions and influences that are expressed in policy developments, explore what underpins and maintains particular structures and interrogate the power relations inherent within them. Relationships between policy, change and research in education are also equally complex. We have seen that the contemporary reforms of education in the United Kingdom have to a large extent had a limited impact in terms of facilitating 'real' advances towards a more equitable and improved physical education in England and Wales. Whether teachers and researchers can now counter, contest, resist or progressively adapt and develop these reforms remains to be seen.

Further reading

Gerwitz, S., Ball, S.J. and Bowe, R. (1995) *Markets, Choice and Equity in Education.* Buckingham: Open University Press.

provides further insights into the policy process in education in the context of local management of schools, while:

Taylor, S., Rizvi, F., Lingard, B., and Henry, M. (1997) *Educational Policy and the Politics of Change.* London: Routledge.

provides an interesting comparative account, focusing on events in Australia.

For further development of some of the theoretical concepts that have been central to our discussion and analysis, readers should refer to:

Bernstein, B. (1990) *The Structuring of Pedagogic Discourse. Volume IV Class, Codes and Control.* London: Routledge.
Bernstein, B. (1996) *Pedagogy, Symbolic Control and Identity. Theory, Research, Critique.* London: Taylor and Francis.
Clegg, S.R. (1989) *Frameworks of Power.* London: Sage Publications Ltd.
Hill, M. (1980) *Understanding Social Policy.* Oxford: Basil Blackwell.

and these texts that are good readers on post structuralism:

Best, S. and Kellner, D. (1991) *Postmodern Theory – Critical Interrogations.* London: Macmillan.
Lyon, D. (1994) *Postmodernity.* Buckingham: The Open University Press.

Chapter 8

Politics, policy and progress in physical education

One thing seems certain in physical education, and may well be true of all other subjects, that the louder the surface level noise of innovation and change, the more the deep structures and basic elements of practice seem to remain basically the same. Both our own research and government inspection reports of physical education in schools in England and Wales have indicated that in terms of the curriculum design and content, and the modes of delivering the subject matter of physical education, little has changed since the introduction of ERA in 1988. As we indicated in Chapter 6, perhaps we should not be surprised by this. The 'flexibility' inherent in the requirements for the NCPE intentionally did very little to challenge the existing state of affairs in physical education, alter deep rooted conventions of the subject, or spur innovation. For the most part, the policies and actions of recent British governments seem to have curtailed rather than supported the more innovative aspirations of teachers, and have defined the change that is to occur in narrow, technocratic and managerialist terms. Consequently curriculum provision in physical education in England and Wales still features disproportionate attention to a narrow range of competitive team games, sex differentiated programmes, and teaching characterised by a *limited* range of teaching methods and strategies (Clay 1997b; Evans, Davies and Penney 1996; Mason 1995a, 1995b; OFSTED 1995; OHMCI 1995; Waddington, Malcolm and Cobb 1998). Drawing upon the most recent OFSTED reports on the standards achieved in secondary education, Clay (1997b) specifically identified the 'weak coverage' of dance and outdoor and adventurous activities at key stage 3 as an outstanding concern; noted poor differentiation in some lessons; and the failure of some schemes of work to adequately address progression in learning, and pedagogical issues such as teaching methods and grouping strategies suitable for different classes or circumstances. In this chapter we therefore once again ask how the content and pattern of provision of physical education in England and Wales matches up to the rhetorical commitment made and widely supported in 1988, that the National Curriculum would raise standards in education and would ensure that 'good curriculum practice' was more widely employed (DES 1989a). We also question whether or not the curricula and pedagogies of contemporary physical education are appropriate to the requirements of a post modern age.

In addition to reflecting that shortcomings in the implementation of the NCPE were perhaps to be expected in the light of the arrangements and conditions that we have described in preceding chapters, we highlight that there has been no let up in the demands placed upon teachers, or the conservatism of the policies effecting them. Since the introduction and revision of the National Curriculum for Physical Education, physical education teachers and teacher educators have faced a further barrage of policies and initiatives that have openly sought to further entrench 'sport' in its position of dominance in physical education (see Penney and Harris 1997). The government's policy statement *Sport – Raising the Game* (Department of National Heritage (DNH) 1995) outlined and laid the foundations for many of these developments. We have seen a mix of incentives and pressures for schools to adopt and further promote a focus upon sport, including the promotion of awards to give recognition to those schools deemed to have effective and innovative policies for promoting sport, and less subtle encouragement to adopt this focus, with a move to the inspections of schools being specifically required to address 'the quality and range of games offered as part of the PE curriculum ... together with the provision for sport outside the curriculum' (DNH 1995; see also Penney and Harris 1997). Once again teachers have been marginalised in developments, called upon to react to new demands rather than playing a central part in their construction and development. In many respects they seem to have been actively co-opted in initiatives to aid the development of sport in physical education. Currently debates about further revisions to the National Curriculum in England and Wales are once again gaining momentum. Dearing's (1993) promised and much needed period of stability in education has openly been cut short, if indeed it existed at all. The contexts in which teachers are working remain uncertain, demanding, stressful, and far from conducive to the growth of innovative and reflective practice in physical education or in any other subject of the curriculum. In these circumstances it is not surprising that the reports of 'standards' in the teaching and learning of physical education have read so negatively (see OFSTED 1995; OHMCI 1995; Clay 1997b). Furthermore, many of the reported 'failings' in implementation of the NCPE may be direct reflections of both the gaps and the non-negotiable prescriptions in central government's texts. In particular we point to the significance of the absence of adequate guidance and discussion about how teachers should approach assessment in the NCPE and of the requirements for competitive games to be experienced by all children, at all phases, for most of the time. The most recent OFSTED inspections of physical education at key stages 3 and 4 revealed that 'too many schools have yet to establish clear criteria against which to make assessments' (Clay 1997b: 8) and identified a continuing 'lack of balance' in some key stage 3 programmes 'with for example, an over-concentration on invasion games, such as soccer, rugby, netball or hockey' (ibid.: 6).

Discourses and progress

So what possibilities remain for innovation in schools, for teachers to express their professionalism, expertise and authority in the contexts of physical education? Has the system of classification and framing inherent in the National Curriculum become so constraining, so demanding, that teachers now simply have to deliver what they are told, and do what they may, or may not believe to be in the interests of the pupils in their care? Looking particularly to the future, we need to recall that all texts contain *multiple discourses*, compromises and contradictions, and that the National Curriculum for Physical Education in England and Wales is no exception in this respect. There thus remains at least some potential for discourses currently subordinated by the interests of competitive sport (for example, relating to dance and aesthetics, outdoor and adventure education, and health) to find expression in subsequent readings, and for distinctly 'different' models of physical education to then emerge. In Bernstein's (1990, 1996) terms, the curriculum can still express a different 'message' to that with which we are most familiar, and, in so doing, challenge the forms of classification and the dominant 'voices' prevailing within physical education in schools (see Chapter 3).

In exploring such potential we address the range of discourses that feature within physical education. We illustrate the many different interests and values that potentially could be expressed and promoted by them, should they find a place in physical education either as of equal status alongside, or instead of, the currently dominant restorationist ideals of sport. Again it is important to bear in mind that when considering issues of curriculum change, we need to acknowledge that discourses in physical education and what is ultimately defined as worthwhile knowledge in the subject not only reflect historical practices and individual preferences, but also trends in physical cultures beyond schools. These trends are themselves inextricably connected to socio-economic changes occurring nationally and globally, not least of which is the near universal privileging of competitive team sports as the dominant form of leisure in contemporary popular culture.

A question of sport

Throughout this book we have portrayed 'sport' as the dominant discourse in the NCPE, and the interests of sport as now occupying a highly privileged position in the school curriculum. This trend has continued since the publication of the statutory orders for the NCPE in England and Wales, with further new initiatives centring upon school sport. These have emanated on the one hand from the Conservative government led by John Major, and, on the other, from the perhaps more enlightened (and industrialist sponsored) initiatives of the Youth Sport Trust (YST). Since its launch in 1994 the YST has established itself as a key organisation for the promotion of sport in schools in England and Wales, and particularly in the primary sector. We have seen a range of new 'opportunities' and 'rewards' for the development of school sport. First and foremost the YST has led the development of the 'TOP programmes'. TOP Play has focused on the teaching of 'core skills and fun sport' to 4 to 9-year-olds, while BT TOP Sport has centred on the introduction of sport and games to 7 to 11-year-olds, and TOP Club has involved governing bodies 'customising' their sport to suit particular club structures and needs (English Sports Council (ESC) 1997a, 1997b). Both TOP Play and BT TOP Sport have centred around the provision of bags of equipment and 'activity cards' for use in implementing the programmes, and the introduction of training for individuals (particularly primary teachers) to deliver the programmes. These initiatives have been described by the English Sports Council as 'exciting and far-reaching programmes', with some 10,000 teachers trained to deliver TOP Play and BT TOP Sport and 4,000 schools in 94 local education authorities receiving equipment bags and sets of activity cards (ESC 1997a). At the same time we have also seen the development of more coaching courses for teachers and the growth of 'Sportsmark' and 'Sportsmark Gold' award schemes for secondary schools deemed to be providing a 'quality physical education and sport programme'. 'Coaching for teachers' is seeking to provide 'tailor-made courses for teachers to enable them to develop their coaching skills' and specifically, provide teachers with 'extra training in their chosen sport to enable them to support and develop extra-curricular sport' (ESC 1997b: 3). With respect to the Sportsmark and Sportsmark Gold schemes, it has been instructive to see the marketing potential of these awards, over and above the matter of quality provision, being emphasised by the English Sports Council. For example, the ESC explained that 'In the present educational climate of open enrolment and parental choice, it is important for schools to project a positive image in the local community, and what better way than by gaining a Sportsmark or Sportsmark Gold award?' (ibid.: 7).

It is easy to see the attractions of these initiatives to headteachers operating in a competitive environment in which any mark of distinction may bring recognition that theirs is a 'better school' and consequently attract more pupils and more funding. It is equally easy to understand why, with resources for in-service training in physical education severely limited, and with expertise and confidence, among primary teachers particularly, at an all time low, the provision of training, equipment and teaching materials has been warmly welcomed by teachers in many schools. Sport has stepped in to fill the gaps in both educational provision and the (material and human) resourcing to support it. As these schemes gather momentum there is a pressing need to take a close look at exactly what and whose interests are being promoted and whether in the longer term children's interests will be well served by them. While these initiatives may constitute a useful resource for impoverished and undertrained teachers, at the same time they serve to paper over gaping inadequacies in education. Sport, as the major proponents of the YST initiatives themselves freely acknowledge, can be no compensation for poor quality physical education, even when it adopts or shapes itself upon worthy educational principles and co-opts the teaching profession to advance its ideals. Indeed, it has been stated that the YST materials now being used in primary schools 'are not a substitute for the national curriculum but an additional resource for teachers that can complement the planning for the school physical education programme' (Youth Sport Trust 1996: 11).

In pursuing these concerns we acknowledge that thus far we may have been guilty of talking of sport (just as we may be in talking of physical education) as if it were a unified and homogeneous phenomenon devoid of internal differences of interest, value and purpose. We therefore stress that, as in our analysis of physical education, we need to consider that in sport there are different interests, ideologies and values at play, and that we are addressing another contested domain. On several occasions we have pointed to the *particular* interpretation and emphasis of 'sport' in the context of the NCPE. Specifically, the defining focus has been upon performance, selection, competition and 'traditional' (Anglo-centric/male) team games. But there are other ways of looking at sport. The emphases, direction and boundaries for 'sport' need not be these, and some developments in physical education in recent years have served to demonstrate the capacity for different values and interests to be explored in initiatives which reach out to different, perhaps more collaborative cultures and worthy educational ideals. For example, 'Teaching Games for Understanding' (TGFU) (see Bunker and Thorpe 1982; Thorpe, Bunker and Almond 1986) and more recently 'Sport Education' (see Alexander, Taggart and Thorpe 1996) initiatives have been characterised by a commitment to position an educational discourse, and children, centrally in the teaching of physical education, albeit through the mediums of games and sport. Both represent avenues that teachers could explore in their delivery of the NCPE, and potentially offer a means of challenging the emphases and interests that are invariably privileged in games dominated curricula. However, although these initiatives may have real merits, they must also be seen as curricula constructed within, and therefore, as potentially 'corrupted' and/or co-opted by, the far narrower interests of cultural restoration and big business sport. None of these developments can therefore be regarded as providing an unproblematic answer to fears of the subordination of educational principles in physical education. They do not necessarily increase momentum towards greater equity in physical education, and in many respects the strengths identified with these initiatives can be seen as the kind of 'good practice' that should be seen *throughout* physical education, not only in the context of sport and games.

For some within physical education, developments such as 'sport education', whatever their pedagogical strengths or weaknesses, represent a distinct threat, rather than positive contribution to, the future of physical education (see for example Talbot 1997; Tinning 1995). The label, 'sport education', over and above the identities and values that may underpin it, seems all important. The reality, of course, is that there are both potential threats and opportunities here in relation to the educational values that are held dear in physical education. Arnold has observed that in recent years 'the phrase "competitive sport" has been used to connote a "serious" undertaking of sport in contradistinction to a "non-serious" or "recreational" approach' (1997: 40). He also reminds us that recreational sport, or participation that emphasises enjoyment, is by no means devoid of competition. In critiquing the serious and elite focus, we are not seeking to remove competition from sport in the context of physical education, but rather to ensure that it is placed in perspective and is consistent with the overriding educational aims, of providing all children with opportunities to develop skills, understanding and a sense of worth as participants in sport. As Arnold explains 'For many schoolchildren (as well as adults) winning is a prospect rarely achieved but this does not prevent them wanting and continuing to compete and trying to win. Their reason for playing may be to do with fun, fitness, therapy, friendship, sociability, or the pursuit of excellence' (1997: 37), and our concern as physical educators should be to attempt to foster and cater for this full spectrum of interests.

Thus whatever new initiative we choose to adopt, it will have the capacity to either nurture or suppress radical or conservative practices. Ultimately the key issues may well be the intention and the purposes that the curriculum is intended to serve, and the quality of the pedagogy, rather than the nature of the content (the type of activity) that pupils experience and receive. Thus we stress that critical issues to address are what discourses initiatives are connecting with, and whether or not they foster progressive or regressive practices. Where do the discourses come from, i.e. how are they located in wider regimes of truth and understanding? Are they set in contexts of inequality and do they then challenge or reinforce those inequalities? In short, we need to repeatedly ask whose voices, whose physical cultures, what forms of corporeality are allowed to find expression and are permitted to be heard in physical education.

A matter of health

This type of critical outlook is needed in considering all initiatives promoted within physical education, not only those primarily concerned with sport. For example, 'health' has similarly been referred to, by ourselves and others, as 'a lobby group' and can be portrayed somewhat artificially as a homogeneous collection of individuals and interests. The reality is very different, and developments in the UK in recent years have served to highlight the diversity of interests and the political struggles that are ongoing within this group. Most notably, we have seen a shift in emphasis from the promotion of health related fitness (HRF) to a focus upon health related exercise (HRE) in schools, reflecting changes in opinion about health and exercise occurring in wider communities of medicine and health. With this change in terminology there have been attempts to direct attention 'beyond' the testing of physical fitness and towards ways in which various aspects of health and fitness may be addressed more holistically in and through physical education. In turn this has led to debates about what are appropriate modes of delivery for HRE in the NCPE and whether HRE should constitute a distinct unit of work in the curriculum and/or be addressed in the context of teaching some or all of the areas of activity. Some argue for a combination of approaches, recognising that the teaching of HRE as a single unit of work is unlikely to prompt sound understanding of its application and relevance throughout all aspects of physical education, but that such a unit can provide essential reinforcement and clarification of health messages that are being promoted via a 'permeation' model (Harris and Elbourn 1992a). Again, however, we need to recognise that if driven by a discourse of individualism which locates the individual rather than the community or state as the purveyor and guardian of 'the nation's health', HRE has the potential to be a damagingly conservative, rather than a liberating, force in and for physical education.

For many teachers charged with producing and revising National Curriculum requirements, and developing HRE within these, the primary concerns have been pragmatic rather than ideological. The dilemma for these teachers has been how to find time to address what are perceived as additional and not necessarily compatible demands while teaching the programmes of study for the areas of activity. Thus the position of health in relation to the NCPE can be seen as one of increased but still marginal status, subordinate to the areas of activity. It is also notable that while HRE may have moved beyond a medically orientated conceptualisation of fitness/health, it still falls far short of promoting a socio-critical view of health. In these terms the discourses of health within the NCPE stand in marked contrast to some developments elsewhere. For example in Australia students are being encouraged to question the different and often contradictory interpretations of 'health' of individuals, communities, societies and cultures, with which they are faced (see Australian Education Council 1994a; 1994b; and Penney 1998b).

There remain tensions and contradictions between the discourses of sport and health in relation to physical education and neither politicians nor members of physical education professional associations seem particularly eager or able to resolve them when making a case for physical education in schools. Without more time and resources for physical education little can be achieved by teachers either in relation to securing the nation's sporting interests or those relating to health. Neither the compatibility of these interests, nor what a curriculum should and could look like that attempts to address both, have been adequately explored to date. These are matters that we return to below. First, however, it is important to remind ourselves that 'sport' and 'health' comprise not only a collection of (rather than single) discourses, but that they are also not the only discourses at stake and expressed in physical education. There are others with an 'activity' focus, such as 'dance' and 'outdoor education', both of which have suffered marginalisation throughout the development of the NCPE and also in the narrative of our own texts. While the requirements of the National Curriculum are now such that these discourses can to a great extent be excluded from physical education, there is also still important potential for them to remain a focus of attention. There are members of the physical education profession committed to ensuring that these discourses are sustained as areas of activity and that they do contribute towards a balanced physical education. In the words of one commentator, specialised dance teachers are 'a dying breed but a resilient bunch!' (Mortimer 1998: 11). Undoubtedly, however, inadequacies in training, perceived inadequacies in expertise, the absence of support from politicians and the powerful countering vested interests that are present in sport, are all barriers to the spread of these 'alternative' practices and in turn, therefore, to their acceptance and increased status in education and physical education. Nevertheless it is encouraging that more guidance firmly directed towards those inexperienced in this area is appearing (see for example Buckle 1995; Sexton 1997).

In whose interests?

In considering the dilemmas and competing interests inherent in the curriculum and pedagogies of physical education, we emphasise again the need to explore the origins of specific discourses, how they interact with each other, and what and whose interests they legitimate or challenge. However, in centring upon the various interests and identities that play upon and operate within physical education it is also all too easy to overlook *children's voices*, and therefore potentially to miss how pupils too are both carriers and recipients of the discursive practices that define classroom culture and the curricula of physical education. Consequently we need ask how well have their interests and values been represented in the debates and developments of the NCPE? How do their voices interact with the texts of the NCPE? Which children, whose discourses, are being included, overlooked or ignored? What does a curriculum look like that puts all children first? What sort of pedagogies would we then expect to see in physical education teaching? What are we seeking when we talk of 'innovative' and 'progressive' practices in physical education?

All of these questions are certainly easier to ask and frame than they are to answer. For Taylor *et al.* progressivism is characterised by a departure from 'the kind of individualism that has become dominant in recent policies', that is, policies that 'champion individual self-interest over social connectedness and collective well-being' (1997: 153). This links well with Allen's comment that 'What we like about schools and what we want from schools determine and are determined by our views about the sort of individuals we prefer to live with' (1997: 4). Progressiveness, then, is seen as countering the tendencies towards the fragmentation of society. It is about adopting a 'social democratic view of social justice rather than those individualistic views of justice that are derived from liberalism' (Taylor *et al.* 1997: 154). A socio-democratic view acknowledges 'the need to create material circumstances, as well as cultural and political spaces, which enable people to engage effectively in civil life. Such spaces are necessary if attempts to resolve the uneasy tension between equality and difference are to prove effective' (ibid.). Progressive moves in education then, will value equality and difference simultaneously. But how is this to be achieved in the practices of physical education?

Curriculum development and the diversification of teaching methods are not easy tasks to embark upon. Far from it. They demand able, well trained and committed teachers, who have support from colleagues, senior staff in schools, and parents. In contexts that repeatedly marginalise and subordinate educational values, few people may see the potential benefits of the developments we propose. Connell (1985) has stated that the curriculum is a definition of both pupils' learning and teachers' work. Such a statement points to the 'authority' and significance of the curriculum as a shaping device (Bernstein 1971, 1990) but underestimates the important spaces for negotiation, innovation and contestation in curriculum matters and the capacity, in Bernstein's (1996) terms, for the 'message' to contradict and potentially challenge the 'voice' of the curriculum. As we have emphasised above, there is scope for different pedagogies to find expression in physical education even within the delivery of 'traditional', restrictive, restorationist curricula. Connell has similarly stressed that the particular forms that pedagogical practices take cannot be assumed and, furthermore, 'are always being constructed anew' (Connell *et al.* 1982: 100). We also stress that what may be deemed a 'progressive' or certainly 'different' curriculum structure does not guarantee that the pedagogies employed will be more open, democratic and equitable. As Edwards (1995) has emphasised, there is not a simple or automatic relationship between the strength of classification and strength of framing in and of curricula.

Encouragingly, some writers have provided important insights into some of the possibilities to which we elude in relation to the ongoing implementation and possible re-orientation of policy. Mawer (1995) has reminded us that there are elements of the National Curriculum (and particularly within the requirements for its 'delivery'), that are potentially 'progressive' but that are all too often overlooked by those who see its text straightforwardly as only and purely a conservative force. For example, he states that in delivering the National Curriculum 'there is a need for the effective teacher to use a variety of teaching styles and strategies in order not only to achieve the objectives suggested by the end of key stage statements, but also to work towards the National Curriculum cross-curricular competencies' (1995: 196). He points out that in physical education this will mean addressing the development of 'decision-making, problem-solving, and personal and social skills', which may necessitate the use of unfamiliar teaching methods, specifically designed to give pupils/students greater responsibility for and involvement in their own learning, and the teacher adopting 'a more facilitatory and mentoring role'. In a subject noted for its over-reliance on didactic teaching, particularly by men, this may not be very easy to achieve and would constitute a fairly radical move. Usefully Mawer not only provides an insight into strategies that can be used to foster these relationships and roles (including peer support and collaborative approaches; pupil self-appraisal, questioning and problem solving approaches) but also illustrates how the expectations and requirements of the National Curriculum for Physical Education can be met through such approaches. For example, Mawer identifies several requirements that 'may be approached using a guided discovery strategy in which questions are posed to the learner or group that lead them to discover an appropriate correct solution, whether it be a particular mechanical principle in athletics ... or principles of attack and defence in invasion games' (ibid.: 209). Similarly, he identifies a 'divergent problem solving approach' in which pupils have the opportunity 'to discover and produce alternative answers to the question or problem set by the teacher' (ibid.: 211), as a suitable strategy to use in working towards objectives such as the key stage 3 requirements that pupils should be taught to refine movements in gymnastics into increasingly complex sequences, and to develop strategic and tactical skills and understanding in games.

Mawer (1995) also identifies methods of **assessment** that can be integrated and compatible with the above approaches to teaching. These not only signal a marked departure from much existing practice in physical education, but also run counter to the prevailing dominant discourses of assessment which centre on measurement and testing. As Graham has pointed out, the idea that the National Curriculum would be 'test led', with 'examinability' coming before education, was embedded in its texts at its inception, such that now 'The hoops through which children are forced to pass through from the age of five are considered far more important than what passes through them' (1996: 170). This is an emphasis which may have resonated well with the conventional partiality for measurement and testing in physical education. It is thus encouraging that Mawer has emphasised the ongoing nature and value of assessment and the need for pupils to be aware of and actively involved in both the setting of criteria and the recording of their progress.

For some teachers none of these ideas and practices will be new. Rather, what they signal is the promotion, continued development and sharing of the good practice that has developed, albeit slowly and unevenly, in recent years, despite the constraints imposed by central government's reform of education. As well as highlighting shortcomings in provision and implementation, inspections have identified very positive developments in the teaching and learning of physical education (see Clay 1997b). However, debate about what physical education is, what purposes it serves and what values we are seeking to promote in teaching and teacher education, remains both topical and much needed. And if we have learnt anything from history and recent developments, it is that we should neither aim for, nor expect, consensus upon these matters. While some commentators appear to express frustration in stating that in physical education professional representation 'remains fragmented and we still have not achieved the consensus about our subject, nor a means of communicating it effectively' (Talbot 1997: 11), our own view is that there is a need for the many different voices and interests in physical education to receive recognition, consideration and support. Much of this book has highlighted the limitations and dangers of trying to subsume multiple discourses and interests within any one dominant agenda. Our aspiration is for a pedagogy of inclusion rather than exclusion and for a curriculum that celebrates innovation and risk taking while remaining sensitive to the diversity of pupils' needs. This would mean among other things, treating the components of the NCPE more as building blocks, to be constructed in co-operation with others who have interests at stake. The NCPE should not be viewed as an immutable design, nor should the task of construction be seen as something to be undertaken by schools alone.

Pedagogy in practice

Perhaps more than anything else we need more talk of pedagogy in physical education. In 1982 Connell *et al.* stated that 'It is curious that the sociology of education has usually taken the student–teacher relationship, the core of schooling, as given' (Connell *et al.* 1982: 100). More recently Walker, Pick and Macdonald (1991) also noted the limited extent of educational research interest in 'the experience and processes of schooling' and the 'late' arrival of classroom research as a focus of attention. Connell *et al.* (1982) argued that, like all relationships of schooling, the student–teacher relationship exists only as practices that are constantly being reconstructed, and emphasised that the form of the appropriation of knowledge is as important a consideration as the form of educational knowledge. In short, how children and young people 'receive' knowledge is as important in educational terms as what it is they receive. Meanwhile Apple has reminded us that 'The politics of pedagogy does not simply involve how or what one is teaching, but the rights of others who are "being taught" to jointly participate in creating the pedagogical environment' (1993: 159). The implication here is not only that students will play an active role in shaping curriculum content, but also in determining the ways in which it is developed and taught; that they have participatory 'rights' to the pedagogical relations of the classroom, gymnasium or playing field (Evans and Davies 1997).

But are we overly optimistic in thinking that teachers will share or can share in our progressive hopes and ideals? Given the intensification of their workloads and the ever increasing pressures towards accountability to centrally defined criteria, the momentum towards the standardisation of curriculum content and the separation of the determination of that content from the process of teaching, may be welcomed rather than resisted by some teachers facing 'contradictory realities' and 'contradictions in their own consciousness' (Apple 1993: 137). Apple has reported how some teachers in the United States *valued* a 'canned' or 'pre-packaged' curriculum, regarding it as 'a practical and sensible solution to the problem of curriculum time, resources, and "skills"' (ibid.: 139). The choices facing teachers are as awesome as they are unenviable: status and dignity as a professional, with a working life of struggle; or a move towards becoming a technician, delivering the packaged curriculum, forfeiting status, authority and control in education, but perhaps achieving stability and much needed peace of mind.

Concluding comments

In 1993 Graham with Tytler stated that 'The national curriculum is a potent tool for change and for bringing about equality of opportunity.

Its potential is largely unrealised as yet' (p. 132). Our study of the policy process has provided further, albeit modest, insights into the complexities of the process and has identified the different arenas in which action is needed if ideological, structural and economic changes in practice are to arise that will result in a more enlightened, imaginative and equitable physical education. In our view there is an urgent need to respond to the knowledge that market forces are serving to reduce possibilities for the development of more inclusivity in education (see for example Gerwitz *et al.* 1995), and that in England and Wales:

> There is now less equality, more stark contrasts [between schools in the education system] than at any time since the war. Hard cheese if you happen to be a pupil in an under-funded, under-performing inner-city school in the mid 1990s.
>
> (Graham 1996: 177)

At the same time we remain aware that 'progressive change is always precarious because of the presence of oppositional discourses' (Taylor *et al.* 1997: 167), and that while we can both emphasise and celebrate the potential for and value of individual teachers in individual schools pursuing alternative agendas and interests, ultimately, there is also a need for changes in 'the system', not only in schools (Connell 1985). In addition a key concern in any development is how these 'different' and currently subordinated discourses and interests are 'positioned' and defined. Connell (1985) reminds us that all too often 'acceptance' and a 'place' in the curriculum may be achieved by 'new' or 'alternative' initiatives redefining themselves (or being (re-)defined) as part of the hegemonic curriculum. The dominant voice of the curriculum, its principles of classification and framing remain secure and unchallenged (Bernstein 1990, 1996). The real challenge for those with different interests in and new visions for physical education is to redefine that hegemonic curriculum. Once again we have to acknowledge the difficulties and possible barriers inherent in such endeavours, and, in particular, consider how these different discourses and curricula will be received by parents. As Connell *et al.* (1982) have emphasised, the alternatives that parents seek may be quite different to those that we have suggested. They reflect with some irony that:

> The parent who is bitterly regretful in retrospect about having dropped out of school at thirteen, is still very likely to blame him or herself, not the school as an institution. 'The alternative', then, is not something different in quality but more of the same ...
>
> (Connell *et al.* 1982: 60)

Certainly, many parents may look back with some regret to their experiences of physical education and yet still perhaps be seeking a similar curriculum and emphasis for their children.

Hargreaves and Evans (1997) have also reminded us that there are dangers inherent in any discourse, but perhaps particularly in some of those that have dominated political and public commentaries upon education in recent years. They draw attention to the prominence of 'failing' schools and teachers within the discourse of school 'improvement', and the repeated lack of recognition of the professionalism and abilities of teachers and their successes in invariably difficult and demanding situations. In these respects Hargreaves and Evans are critical of the statements that thus far have been forthcoming from the newly elected Labour government in the UK. In their view 'Labour's voice has perhaps echoed too readily the strident tones of Conservative education policy and its preoccupation with celebrating parental choice and eliminating "failing schools"' (1997: 11). They emphasise that 'At a time when teachers and schools have endured years of scapegoating and stigmatization, and when they desperately need to feel they are a valued part of the solution, and not just an obstacle to Reform Act implementation, some signs of positive support and intervention from which teachers might benefit are urgently needed' (ibid.). It is with regret that we also reflect that to date there has been little evidence of such support for physical education in particular; its future in the curricula of schools in England and Wales remains uncertain.

Research in policy and practice in PE

Our hope is that this book will have gone some way towards illustrating the potential contribution that policy research can make to curriculum and pedagogical developments in physical education. Such research has the capacity, in our view, to provide critical and much needed insights into the complexities and inequities of the processes and conditions that many of us experience in either higher education or schools. Indeed we would go further, and say that it has the capacity to inform the thinking of politicians and the actions of teachers in schools. Once again we stress that in order to provide these insights our research has had to feature complexities and uncertainties, and, in particular, to attempt to embrace the multitude of influences, sites and individuals variously shaping policy and practice in education. We hope that others will be inspired to take up some of the challenges that we have presented not only for research in physical education, but perhaps more importantly, for teaching and teacher education in the subject. We remain convinced that unpacking (deconstructing) relationships within and between education and wider socio-cultural arenas is a precursor to knowing better how they are to be put back together in the interests of greater equity and higher quality physical education for all.

Summary

For all the talk of reform in physical education in England and Wales and elsewhere, we can reflect that in important respects very little has changed in the curricula and pedagogies of physical education. Notable inequities have been sustained not only in 'official' policy documents, but also in their implementation. None the less there remains some scope for teachers and others to explore gaps and omissions in official texts, and in particular to utilise varied and alternative pedagogies in teaching physical education. These may express and promote values and interests that are at variance to those currently dominant in the subject. At the same time we emphasise that the potential for either conservatism or progressivism is always present in curriculum frameworks, and recent initiatives and developments centring upon sport offer no exception to this rule. We also note the importance of identifying and locating the *origins* of the discourses when considering the likelihood of policy and curriculum development sponsoring greater equity in physical education. The different and arguably more progressive approaches that we indicate may be employed in the delivery of the National Curriculum for Physical Education in England and Wales may also have to be implemented in contexts of continued pressure, emanating from many sources (including colleagues in schools, parents and politicians) for the maintenance and reinforcement of more traditional emphases and approaches in physical education and the reinforcement of the status quo.

Further reading

As indicated, Mawer's text provides useful discussion of different approaches to the teaching of physical education:

Mawer, M. (1995) *The Effective Teaching of Physical Education*. London: Longman.

In addition, the following edited collections provide further discussion of many contemporary initiatives and issues in physical education:

Armstrong, N. (ed.) (1996) *New Directions in Physical Education. Change and Innovation*. London: Cassell.
Evans, J. (ed.) (1993) *Equality, Education and Physical Education*. London: Falmer Press.

Green, K. and Hardman, K. (eds) (1998) *Physical Education: A Reader*. Aachen, Germany: Meyer & Meyer.

McFee, G. and Tomlinson, A. (eds) (1993) *Education, Sport, Leisure: Connections and Controversies*. Eastbourne: Chelsea School Research Centre, University of Brighton.

Appendix A: Outline of research sites and methods

The research that we undertook during the period 1990–1995 attempted to operate simultaneously at multiple 'levels' (national government, local government, and schools) of the education system, and employed a range of methods within a qualitative and ethnographic framework. In our investigation of the development and implementation of the National Curriculum for Physical Education every effort was made to keep pace with developments at all levels at all times. Inherent in our design, therefore, was the flexibility to be able to accommodate unforeseen developments in the policy process and to take up opportunities arising for access to particular research sites and/or individuals. Thus while developments centring upon national government, local government, and schools were each our primary focus of attention at particular times, our design sought to avoid a rigid sequential pattern of investigation and always to retain contact with all levels, albeit with a reduced emphasis. Here we provide an outline of the sites explored and methods used. For further discussion of methodological issues see Evans and Penney (1992) and Penney (1994).

Documentary research

- Central government texts (National Curriculum; National Curriculum for Physical Education; other policies within the ERA).
- Local government texts (National Curriculum; National Curriculum for Physical Education; physical education more generally; other policies within the ERA).
- Texts produced by physical education professional associations and other organisations with interests in physical education (National Curriculum for Physical Education).
- School and physical education department texts (from case study schools, see below) (National Curriculum; National Curriculum for Physical Education; Physical Education more generally; other policies within the ERA).

Participant observation

- Consultation/dissemination meetings/conferences organised by curriculum agencies in England and in Wales (National Curriculum; National Curriculum for Physical Education).
- Consultation meetings held within case study Local Education Authorities (one LEA in England was the focus for our investigations 1990–1993; a different LEA in England and an LEA in Wales were our focus during 1994–5) (National Curriculum; National Curriculum for Physical Education; Physical Education more generally).
- In-service training courses organised by case study LEAs (National Curriculum; National Curriculum for Physical Education; physical education more generally).
- Meetings of physical education inspectors within the case study LEAs.
- Consultation meetings organised by professional associations nationally and regionally (National Curriculum; National Curriculum for Physical Education).
- Regional meetings of physical education professional associations.
- Physical education in case study schools (7 schools within the case study LEA in England 1990–1993; 3 schools in one LEA in England and 3 schools in one LEA in Wales 1994–5).

Semi-structured interviews

- Members of the National Curriculum for Physical Education working group.
- Representatives of the case study Local Education Authorities.
- Headteachers, heads of physical education, physical education teachers and other staff (e.g. deputy headteacher) in case study schools.

Questionnaire surveys

- Headteachers and heads of physical education in all state secondary schools within the case study LEA in England 1991.
- Heads of physical education in all state primary, middle and secondary schools within the case study LEA in England 1994.

Appendix B: Local Education Authority documentation

LEA (1990a) Local Management of Schools: The Seashire[1] Scheme. A Summary Guide.

LEA (1990b) Local Management of Schools: Seashire's Scheme. Briefing Information for Heads and Governors.

LEA (1991a) Response from the teachers and inspectors in Seashire to the Secretary of State's proposals for Physical Education 5-16 in the DES/Welsh Office NCC Consultation document – August 1991.

LEA (1991b) The response from Seashire teachers to the National Curriculum Physical Education Working Group Interim Report.

LEA (1991c) The Use of Time in Secondary Schools – Timetabling the Secondary Curriculum.

---

1 'Seashire' is the pseudonym used for the LEA upon which our research centred 1990–1993.

References

Aldrich, R. (1995) 'Educational Reform and Curriculum Implementation in England: An Historical Perspective', in D.S.G. Carter, and M.H. O'Neill, (eds) *International Perspectives on Educational Reform and Policy Implementation*. London: Falmer Press.

Alexander, K., Taggart, A. and Thorpe, S. (1996) 'A Spring in their Steps? Possibilities for Professional Renewal through Sport Education in Australian Schools', *Sport, Education and Society* 1(1): 5–22.

Allen, G. (1997) *Education at Risk*. London: Cassell.

Almond, L. and Harris, J. (1997) 'The ABC of H.R.E.', *British Journal of Physical Education* 28(3): 14–16.

Apple, M.W. (1982) *Education and Power*. London: Ark Paperbacks.

Apple, M.W. (1993) 'Official Knowledge', London: Routledge.

Armstrong, N. (ed.) (1996) *New Directions in Physical Education. Change and Innovation*. London: Cassell.

Armstrong, N. and Sparkes, A. (eds) (1991) *Issues in Physical Education*. London: Cassell.

Arnold, P.J. (1997) *Sport, Ethics and Education*. London: Cassell.

Atkinson, P., Davies, B. and Delamont, S. (eds) (1995) *Discourse and Reproduction. Essays in Honor of Basil Bernstein*. New Jersey: Hampton Press.

Australian Education Council (AEC) (1994a) *A Statement on Health and Physical Education for Australian Schools*. Carlton, Victoria: Curriculum Corporation.

Australian Education Council (AEC) (1994b) *Health and Physical Education – a Curriculum Profile for Australian Schools*. Carlton, Victoria: Curriculum Corporation.

Awdurdod Cwricwlwm Asesu Cymru (Curriculum and Assessment Authority for Wales) (ACAC) (1994) *Physical Education in the National Curriculum. Proposals for Consultation under Section 242 of the Education Act 1993*. Cardiff: ACAC.

BAALPE (1991a) 'The Response of the British Association of Advisers and Lecturers in Physical Education to the National Curriculum Physical Education Working Group Interim Report', unpublished paper, BAALPE.

BAALPE (1991b) 'The response from the British Association of Advisers and Lecturers in Physical Education to the Secretary of State's proposals for Physical Education 5–16', unpublished paper, BAALPE.

Ball, S.J. (1990a) *Markets, Morality and Equality in Education. Hillcole Group Paper 5.* London: Tufnell Press.

Ball, S.J. (1990b) *Politics and Policy Making in Education. Explorations in Policy Sociology.* London: Routledge.

Ball, S.J. (1993a) 'Education Policy, Power Relations and Teachers' work', *British Journal of Educational Studies* XXXXI(2): 106–121.

Ball, S.J. (1993b) 'What is Policy? Texts, Trajectories and Toolboxes', *Discourse, Studies in the Cultural Politics of Education* 13(1): 10–17.

Ball, S.J. (1997) 'Policy Sociology and Critical Social Research: a personal review of recent education policy and policy research', *British Educational Research Journal* 23(3): 257–274.

Barber, M. and Graham, D. (eds) (1993) *Sense, Nonsense and the National Curriculum.* London: Falmer Press.

BCPE (1990) *The National Curriculum in Physical Education* London: BCPE.

BCPE (1991) 'Response of the British Council of Physical Education to the National Curriculum Physical Education Working Group Interim Report', unpublished paper, BCPE.

Beer, I. (1991) 'Letter to Kenneth Clarke', in DES and WO *National Curriculum Physical Education Working Group Interim Report.* London: DES.

Bernstein, B. (1971) 'On the Classification and Framing of Educational Knowledge', in M.F.D. Young (ed.) *Knowledge and Control. New Directions for the Sociology of Education.* London: Collier Macmillan.

Bernstein, B. (1990) *The Structuring of Pedagogic Discourse. Volume IV Class, Codes and Control.* London: Routledge.

Bernstein, B. (1996) *Pedagogy, Symbolic Control and Identity. Theory, Research, Critique.* London: Taylor & Francis.

Best, S. and Kellner, D. (1991) *Postmodern Theory – Critical Interrogations.* London: Macmillan.

BISC (1991) 'The Response of the British Institute of Sports Coaches to the Interim Report of the National Curriculum Physical Education Working Group', *Sportscoach* (May): 11.

Bowe, R. and Ball, S.J. with Gold, A. (1992) *Reforming Education and Changing Schools. Case Studies in Policy Sociology.* London: Routledge.

Brown, S. (1991) 'Effective Contributions from Research to Educational Conventions: Style and Strategy', *British Educational Research Journal* 17(1): 5–18.

Buckle, D. (1995) 'National Curriculum: The Teaching of Dance', *British Journal of Physical Education* 26(3): 16–20.

Bunker, D.J. and Thorpe, R.D. (1982) 'A Model for the Teaching of Games in the Secondary School', *Bulletin of Physical Education* 10: 9–16.

Carter, D.S.G. (1995) 'Curriculum Reform and the Neo-corporist State in Australia', in D.S.G. Carter and M.H. O'Neill (eds) *International Perspectives on Educational Reform and Policy Implementation.* London: Falmer Press.

Carter, D.S.G. and O'Neill, M.H. (eds) (1995) *International Perspectives on Educational Reform and Policy Implementation.* London: Falmer Press.

CCPR (1991) 'Response to the National Curriculum Physical Education Interim Report', unpublished paper, CCPR.

Clarke, K. (1991) 'Letter to Ian Beer', in DES and WO *National Curriculum Physical Education Working Group Interim Report*. London: DES.

Clay, G. (1997a) 'Standards in Primary Physical Education: OFSTED 1995–97', *Primary PE Focus* (Autumn): 4–6.

Clay, G. (1997b) 'Standards in Primary and Secondary Physical Education: OFSTED 1995–96', *British Journal of Physical Education* 28(2): 5–9.

Clegg, S.R. (1989) *Frameworks of Power*. London: Sage Publications Ltd.

Connell, R.W. (1985) *Teachers' Work*. London: Allen & Unwin.

Connell, R.W., Ashenden, D.J., Kessler, S. and Dowsett, G.W. (1982) *Making the Difference. Schools, Families and Social Division*. London: Allen & Unwin.

Crutchley, D.H. and Robinson, L. (1996) 'Teachers' Perceptions of "Planning", "Performing" and "Evaluating" within National Curriculum Physical Education', *The Bulletin of Physical Education* 32(1): 46–54.

Curtner-Smith, M.D., Kerr, I.G. and Hencken, C.L. (1995) 'The Impact of the National Curriculum Physical Education on Teachers' Behaviours Related with Pupils' Skill Learning: A Case Study in One English Town', *British Journal of Physical Education Research Supplement* 16(Summer): 2–12.

Cyngor Cwricwlwm Cymru (Curriculum Council for Wales) (CCW) (1992) *Physical Education in the National Curriculum. Non-Statutory Guidance for Teachers*. Cardiff: CCW.

CCW (1994a) *A Curriculum Leader's Guide to Physical Education in the National Curriculum at KS1 and KS2*. Cardiff: CCW.

CCW (1994b) *A Teacher's Guide to Physical Education in the National Curriculum at KS3*. Cardiff: CCW.

Dale, R.(1992) 'What Do They Know of England Who Don't Know They've Been Speaking Prose', paper presented at ESRC Research Seminar on Methodological and Ethical Issues Associated with Research into the 1988 Education Reform Act, University of Warwick, 29 April.

Dale, R. and Robertson, S. (1997) '"Resiting" the Nation, "Reshaping the State". Globalisation Effects on Education Policy in New Zealand', in M. Olssen and K. Morris Matthews (eds) *Education Policy in New Zealand: The 1990s and Beyond*. Palmerston North, New Zealand: Dunmore Press.

Davies, A.M., Holland, J. and Minhas, R. (1990) *Equal Opportunities in the New ERA. Hillcole Group Paper 2*. London: Tufnell Press.

Davies, B., Evans, J., Penney, D. and Bass, D. (1997) 'Physical education and nationalism in Wales', *The Curriculum Journal* 8(2): 249–270.

Dearing, R. (1993) *The National Curriculum and its Assessment. Final Report*. London: SCAA.

Department of Education and Science (DES) (1988) 'E.R.A.: L.M.S.' *Circular No. 7/88*. London: DES.

DES (1989a) *National Curriculum – From Policy to Practice*. London: DES.

DES (1989b) 'Education Reform Act 1988. Charges for School Activities', *Circular No. 2/89*. London: DES.

DES (1990) 'John MacGregor Announces Physical Education Working Group', DES press paper 11 July.

DES and Welsh Office (WO) (1991a) *National Curriculum Physical Education Working Group Interim Report*. London: DES.

DES and WO (1991b) *Physical Education for Ages 5–16. Proposals of the Secretary of State for Education and the Secretary of State for Wales*. London: DES.

DES and WO (1992) *Physical Education in the National Curriculum*. London: DES.

Department for Education (DFE) and WO (1995) *Physical Education in the National Curriculum*. London: DFE.

Department of National Heritage (DNH) (1995) *Sport – Raising the Game*. London: DNH.

Dudley, J. and Vidovich, L. (1995) *The Politics of Education Commonwealth Schools Policy 1973–95*. Melbourne, Australia: The Australian Council for Educational Research Ltd.

Edwards, A.D. (1995) 'Changing Pedagogic Discourse', in P. Atkinson, B. Davies and S. Delamont (eds) *Discourse and Reproduction. Essays in Honor of Basil Bernstein*. New Jersey: Hampton Press Inc.

English Sports Council (ESC) (1997a) *National Junior Sport Programme News* (March). London: ESC.

ESC (1997b) *Annual Report 1996–7*. London: ESC.

Evans, J. (1986) (ed.) *Physical Education, Sport and Schooling. Studies in the Sociology of Physical Education*. London: Falmer Press.

Evans, J. (1990) 'Defining a Subject: The Rise and Rise of the New PE?', *British Journal of Sociology of Education* 11(2): 155–169.

Evans, J. (ed.) (1993) *Equality, Education and Physical Education*. London: Falmer Press.

Evans, J. and Davies, B. (1993) 'Equality, Equity and Physical Education', in J. Evans (ed.) *Equality, Education and Physical Education*. London: Falmer Press.

Evans, J. and Davies, B. (1997) 'Editorial Introduction. Physical Education, Sport and the Curriculum', *The Curriculum Journal* 8(2): 185–197.

Evans, J., Davies, B. and Penney, D. (1994) 'Whatever Happened to the Subject and the State in Policy Research in Education', *Discourse: Studies in the Cultural Politics of Education* 14(2): 57–64.

Evans, J., Davies, B. and Penney, D. (1996) 'Teachers, Teaching and the Social Construction of Gender Relations', *Sport, Education and Society* 1(2): 165–183.

Evans, J. and Penney, D. (1992) 'Investigating ERA: Qualitative Methods and Policy Orientated Research', *British Journal of Physical Education, Research Supplement* 11: 2–7.

Evans, J. and Penney, D. (1994) 'Whatever Happened to Good Advice? Service and Inspection after the Education Reform Act', *British Educational Research Journal* 20(5): 519–533.

Evans, J. and Penney, D. (1995a) 'Physical Education, Restoration and the Politics of Sport', *Curriculum Studies* 3(2): 183–196.

Evans, J. and Penney, D. (1995b) 'The Politics of Pedagogy: Making a National Curriculum Physical Education', *Journal of Education Policy* 10(1): 27–44.

Finch, J. (1986) *Research and Policy. The Uses of Qualitative Methods in Social and Educational Research*. London: Falmer Press.

Foster, E. and Bathmaker, A. (1993) 'Equal Opportunities and the National Curriculum', in M. Barber and D. Graham (eds) *Sense, Nonsense and the National Curriculum*. London: Falmer Press.

Foucault, M. (1972) *The Archaeology of Knowledge* (A. Sheridan-Smith, trans.). New York: Harper.

Foucault, M. (1977) *Language, Counter-Memory, Practice* (D. Bouchard, trans.). Oxford: Basil Blackwell.

Foucault, M. (1980) *Power/Knowledge* (C. Gordon, ed., C. Gordon, L. Marshall, J. Mephan and K. Soper, trans.). New York: Pantheon.

Fox, K. (1992) 'Education for Exercise and the National Curriculum Proposals: A Step Forwards or Backwards', *British Journal of Physical Education* 23(1): 8–11.

Gerwitz, S., Ball, S.J. and Bowe, R. (1995) *Markets, Choice and Equity in Education*. Buckingham: Open University Press.

Giddens, A. (1979) *Central Problems in Social Theory, Action, Structure and Contradiction in Social Analysis*. London: Macmillan Press.

Goodson, I. (1991) 'On Understanding Curriculum: The Alienation of Curriculum Theory', in I. Goodson and R. Walker (eds) *Biography, Identity and Schooling. Episodes in Educational Research*. London: Falmer Press.

Goodson, I.(1993) *School Subjects and Curriculum Change. Studies in Curriculum History* (3rd edn) London: Falmer Press.

Grace, G. (1984) *Education and the City: Theory, History and Contemporary Practice*. London: Routledge.

Graham, D. (1996) *The Education Racket*. Glasgow: Neil Wilson Publishing.

Graham, D. with Tytler, D. (1993) *A Lesson for Us All. The Making of the National Curriculum*. London: Routledge.

Green, K. and Hardman, K. (eds) (1998) *Physical Education: A Reader*. Aachen, Germany: Meyer and Meyer.

Halpin, D. and Troyna, B. (eds) (1994) *Researching Education Policy. Ethical and Methodological Issues*. London: Falmer Press.

Ham, C. and Hill, M. (1984) *The Policy Process in the Modern Capitalist State*. London: Wheatsheaf Books Ltd.

Hammersley, M. (1994) 'Ethnography, Policy Making and Practice in Education', in D. Halpin and B. Troyna (eds) *Researching Education Policy. Ethical and Methodological Issues*. London: Falmer Press.

Hargreaves, A. (1986) 'The Macro–Micro Problem in the Sociology of Education', in M. Hammersley (ed.) *Controversies in Classroom Research*. Buckingham: Open University Press.

Hargreaves, A and Evans, R. (1997) 'Teachers and Educational Reform', in A. Hargreaves and R. Evans (eds) *Beyond Educational Reform. Bringing Teachers Back In*. Buckingham: Open University Press.

Harris, J. and Cale, L. (1998) 'Activity Promotion in Physical Education', in K. Green and K. Hardman (eds) *Physical Education – A Reader*. Aachen, Germany: Meyer & Meyer Publishing.

Harris, J. and Elbourn, J. (1992a) 'Highlighting Health Related Exercise within the National Curriculum – Part 1', *British Journal of Physical Education* 23(1): 18–22.

Harris, J. and Elbourn, J. (1992b) 'Highlighting Health Related Exercise within the National Curriculum – Part 2', *British Journal of Physical Education* 23(2): 5–9.

HEA/PEA (1991) 'Summary of the Response to the National Curriculum Physical Education Working Group Interim Report', *HEA Health and Physical Education Project Newsletter* 27: 2–5.

Henry, M. (1993) 'What is Policy? A response to Stephen Ball', *Discourse, Studies in the Cultural Politics of Education* 14(1): 102–105.

Hill, M. (1980) *Understanding Social Policy*. Oxford: Basil Blackwell.

Hoyle, E. (1986) *The Politics of School Management*. London: Hodder & Stoughton.

Jones, S. (1994) 'Welcome Kick in the Right Direction', *Sunday Times* (10 April): 8.

Kay, W. (1998) 'The New Right and Physical Education: A Critical Analysis', Doctoral thesis, Loughborough University.

Kelly, A.V. (1990) *The National Curriculum. A Critical Review*. London: Paul Chapman Publishing Ltd.

Kennedy, K.J. (1995) 'An Analysis of the Policy Contexts of Recent Curriculum Reform Efforts in Australia, Great Britain and the United States', in D.S.G. Carter and M.H. O'Neill (eds) *International Perspectives on Educational Reform and Policy Implementation*. London: Falmer Press.

Kirk, D. (1992) *Defining Physical Education: The Social Construction of a School Subject in Postwar Britain*. London: Falmer Press.

Lawton, D. (1993) 'Is There Coherence and Purpose in the National Curriculum?', in B. Simon and C. Chitty (eds) *Education Answers Back. Critical Responses to Government Policy*. London: Lawrence & Wishart Ltd.

Lingard, R. (1993) 'The Changing State of Policy Production in Education: Some Australian Reflections on the State of Policy Sociology', paper presented to the International Sociology of Education Conference, University of Sheffield, 4–6 January.

The LMS Initiative (1990) *Local Management in Schools: A Practical Guide* (2nd edn). London: The Local Management in Schools Initiative.

Luke, A. (1995) 'Text and Discourse in Education: An Introduction to Critical Discourse Analysis', in M. Apple (ed.) *Review of Research in Education*. Washington: American Educational Research Association

Lukes, S. (1974) *Power: A Radical View*. London: Macmillan Press.

Lundgren, Ulf. P. (1977) *Model Analysis of Pedagogical Processes*. Stockholm: Stockholm Institute of Education/CWK Gleerup.

Lyon, D. (1994) *Postmodernity*. Buckingham: Open University Press.

McFee, G. and Tomlinson, A. (eds) (1993) *Education, Sport, Leisure: Connections and Controversies*. Eastbourne: Chelsea School Research Centre, University of Brighton.

Maclure, S. (1989) *Education Re-formed. A Guide to the Education Reform Act* (2nd edition). London: Hodder & Stoughton.

McNab, T. (1992) 'The Leshbok are Moving', *SportsCoach* (March): 4–5.

Marsh, C.J. (1994) *Producing a National Curriculum*. Australia: Allen & Unwin.

Marston, P. and Jones, G. (1994) 'Teachers Take Sides in School Sports Debate', *Daily Telegraph* 9 April.

Mason, V. (1995a) *Young People and Sport in England, 1994*. London: The Sports Council.

Mason, V. (1995b) *Young People and Sport in England, 1994. The Views of Teachers and Children*. London: The Sports Council.

Maw, J. (1993) 'The National Curriculum Council and the Whole Curriculum: Reconstruction of a Discourse?', *Curriculum Studies* 1(1): 55–73.

Mawer, M. (1995) *The Effective Teaching of Physical Education*. London: Longman.

Mortimer, K. (1998) 'Dance in Education: Process v Product – A Balancing Act!', *British Journal of Physical Education* 29(1): 11–14.

Murdoch, E.B. (1992) 'Physical Education Today', *The Bulletin of Physical Education* 28(2): 15–24.

NCC (1990) *The Whole Curriculum*. York: NCC.

NCC (1991) *Physical Education in the National Curriculum. A Report to the Secretary of State for Education and Science on the Statutory Consultation for the Attainment Target and Programmes of Study in Physical Education*. York: NCC.

NCF (1991) 'Response of the National Coaching Foundation to the Interim Report of the National Curriculum Physical Education Working Group', unpublished paper, NCF.

Office for Standards in Education (OFSTED) (1995) *Physical Education. A Review of Inspection Findings 1993/4*. London: HMSO.

Office of Her Majesty's Chief Inspector of Schools in Wales (OHMCI) (1995) *Report by HM Inspectors. Survey of Physical Education in Key Stages 1, 2 and 3*. Cardiff: OHMCI.

Pascall, D. (1991) 'Letter to Kenneth Clarke', in NCC *Physical Education in the National Curriculum. A Report to the Secretary of State for Education and Science on the Statutory Consultation for the Attainment Target and Programmes of Study in Physical Education*. York: NCC.

PEA (1991) 'The Response by the Physical Education Association to the National Curriculum Physical Education Interim Report', unpublished paper, PEA.

Penney, D. (1994) '"NO CHANGE IN A NEW ERA?" The Impact of the Education Reform Act (1988) on the Provision of PE and Sport in State Schools', PhD thesis, University of Southampton.

Penney, D. (1998a) 'School Subjects and Structures: Reinforcing Traditional Voices in Contemporary "reforms" of education', *Discourse, Studies in the Cultural Politics of Education* 19(1): 5–18.

Penney, D. (1998b) 'Positioning and Defining Physical Education, Sport and Health in the Curriculum', *European Physical Education Review* 4(2): 104–116.

Penney, D. and Evans, J. (1991) 'The Impact of the Education Reform Act (ERA) on the Provision of Physical Education and Sport in the 5–16 Curriculum of State Schools', *British Journal of Physical Education* 22(1): 38–42.

Penney, D. and Evans, J. (1994) 'It's Just Not (and Not Just) Cricket', *British Journal of Physical Education* 25(3): 9–12.

Penney, D. and Evans, J. (1996) 'When Breadth and Balance means Balancing the Books: Curriculum Planning in Schools post-ERA', in C. Pole and R. Chawla (eds) *Educational Change in the 1990s: Perspectives on Secondary Schooling*. London: Falmer Press.

Penney, D. and Glover, S. (1998) 'Contested Identities: A Comparative Analysis of the Position and Definitions of Physical Education in National Curriculum

Developments in England and Wales and Australia', *European Journal of Physical Education* 3(1): 5–21.

Penney, D. and Harris, J. (1997) 'Extra-Curricular Physical Education: More of the Same for the More Able?', *Sport, Education and Society* 2(1): 41–54.

Raab, C.D. (1994) 'Where We Are Now: Reflections on the Sociology of Education Policy', in D. Halpin and B. Troyna (eds) *Researching Education Policy. Ethical and Methodological Issues*. London: Falmer Press.

Ranson, S. (1985) 'Changing Relations between Centre and Locality in Education', in I. McNay and J. Ozga (eds) *Policy-making in Education. The Breakdown of Consensus*. Oxford: Pergamon Press.

Ranson, S. (1986) 'Power Relations in that New Structure', in S. Ranson and J. Tomlinson (eds) *The Changing Government of Education*. London: Allen & Unwin.

Reynolds, D. (1989) 'Better Schools? Present and Potential Policies about the Goals, Organisation and Management of Secondary Schools', in A. Hargreaves and D. Reynolds (eds) *Education Policies: Controversies and Critiques*. London: Falmer Press.

Sabatier, P.A. (1993) 'Top-down and Bottom-up Approaches to Implementation Research', in M. Hill (ed.) *The Policy Process: A Reader*. London: Harvester Wheatsheaf.

Sadovnik, A. (1995) 'Basil Bernstein's Theory of Pedagogic Practice: A Structuralist Approach', in A. Sadovnik (ed.) *Knowledge and Pedagogy. The Sociology of Basil Bernstein*. New Jersey: Ablex Publishing Co.

SCAA (1994a) *Physical Education in the National Curriculum. Draft Proposals*. London: SCAA.

SCAA (1994b) *The Review of the National Curriculum: A Report on the 1994 Consultation*. London: SCAA.

SCOPE (1991a) 'SCOPE Response to the Physical Education Working Group Interim Report', unpublished paper, SCOPE.

SCOPE (1991b) 'Response to the Secretary of State's Proposals for Physical Education 5–16', unpublished paper, SCOPE.

Sexton, K. (1997) 'Oh No its the Dance Block!!', *British Journal of Physical Education* 28(3): 5–8.

Shaughnessy, J. and Price, L. (1995a) 'Physical Education in Primary Schools. A Whole New Ball Game', *The Bulletin of Physical Education* 31(1): 14–20.

Shaughnessy, J. and Price, L. (1995b) 'Physical Education in Primary Schools. What's been going on since September 1992?', *The Bulletin of Physical Education* 31(2): 34–42.

Shilling, C. (1993) 'The Body, Class and Social Inequalities', in J. Evans (ed.) *Equality, Education and Physical Education*. London: Falmer Press.

Simon, B. (1988) *Bending the Rules. The Baker 'Reform' of Education*. London: Lawrence & Wishart Ltd.

Smart, B. (1983) *Foucault, Marxism and Critique*. London: Routledge & Kegan Paul.

Sparkes, A.C. (1992) 'Writing and the Textual Construction of Realities: Some Challenges for Alternative Paradigms Research in Physical Education', in

A.C. Sparkes (ed.) *Research in Physical Education and Sport: Exploring Alternative Visions*. London: Falmer Press.

Sullivan, K. (1997) 'They've Opened Pandora's Box: Educational Reform, the New Right and Teachers' Ideologies', in M. Olssen and K. Morris Matthews (eds) *Education Policy in New Zealand: The 1990s and Beyond*. Palmerston North, New Zealand: The Dunmore Press.

Talbot, M. (1992) 'Sport and Dance in School', *Sport and Leisure* (March/April): 14–15.

Talbot, M. (1993) 'Physical Education and the National Curriculum: Some Political Issues', in G. McFee and A. Tomlinson (eds) *Education, Sport and Leisure: Connections and Controversies*. Eastbourne: Chelsea School Research Centre, University of Eastbourne.

Talbot, M. (1997) 'Values and Aspirations for the Profession', *The Bulletin of Physical Education* 33(3): 6–23.

Taylor, S. (1997) 'Critical Policy Analysis: Exploring Contexts, Texts and Consequences', *Discourse: Studies in the Cultural Politics of Education*, 18(1): 23–35.

Taylor, S., Rizvi, F., Lingard, B., and Henry, M. (1997) *Educational Policy and the Politics of Change*. London: Routledge.

Thorpe, R.D., Bunker, D.J. and Almond, L. (1986) *Rethinking Games Teaching*. Loughborough: Department of Physical Education and Sports Science, Loughborough University.

Tinning, R. (1995) 'The Sport Education Movement: A Phoenix, Bandwagon or Hearse for Physical Education?', *The ACHPER Healthy Lifestyles Journal* 42(4): 19–20.

Troyna, B. (1994) 'Reforms, Research and Being Reflexive About Being Reflective', in D. Halpin and B. Troyna (eds) *Researching Education Policy. Ethical and Methodological Issues*. London: Falmer Press.

Waddington, I., Malcolm, D. and Cobb, J. (1998) 'Gender Stereotyping and Physical Education', *European Physical Education Review* 4(1): 34–46.

Walker, R., Pick, C. and Macdonald, B. (1991) '"Other Rooms: Other Voices" – A Dramatized Report', in I. Goodson and R. Walker (eds) *Biography, Identity and Schooling. Episodes in Educational Research*. London: Falmer Press.

Wallace, M. (1998) 'A Counter-policy to Subvert Education Reform? Collaboration among Schools and Colleges in a Competitive Climate', *British Educational Research Journal* 24(2): 195–216.

Walsh, A. (1992) 'Champion Coaching Project', *British Journal of Physical Education* 23(3): 21–23.

Whitty, G. (1997) 'Education, Policy and the Sociology of Education', *International Studies in Sociology of Education* 7(2): 121–137.

Wood, N. (1994) 'Major Called In to Umpire Dispute Over School Sports', *The Times* (9 April): 7.

Wyatt, J. (1993) 'Delivering the National Curriculum – An L.E.A. Perspective', *The Bulletin of Physical Education* 29(1): 12–14.

Youth Sport Trust (1996) 'TOP Opportunities for Primary Schools', *Primary PE Focus* (Spring): 11–14.

Index